THE Dave Myers and Si King
HAIRY
BIKERS
RIDE AGAIN

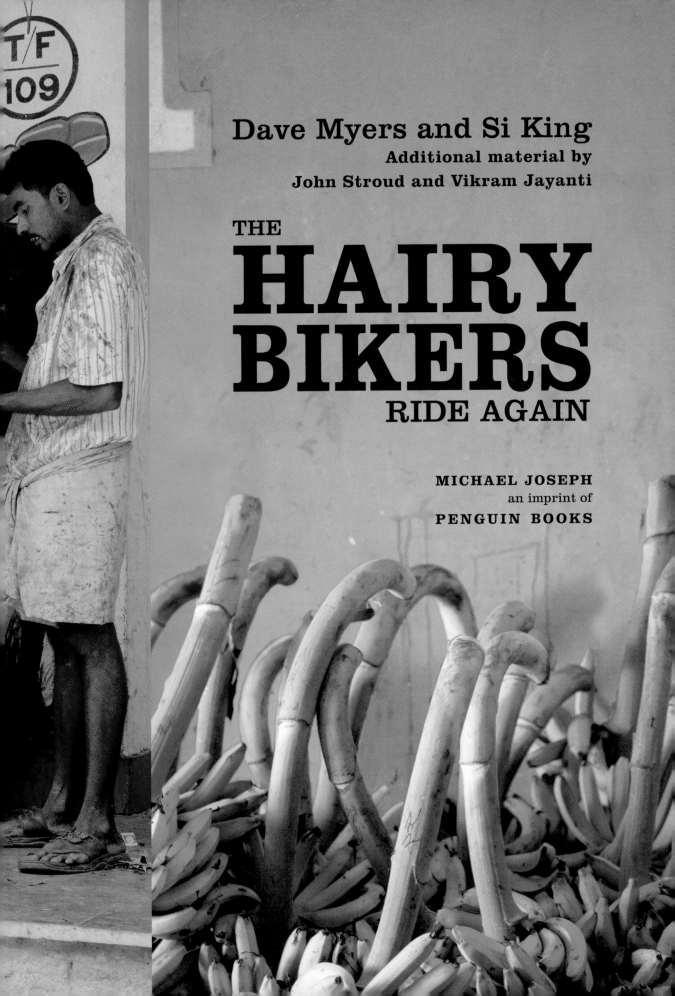

Dave Myers and Si King
Additional material by
John Stroud and Vikram Jayanti

THE
HAIRY
BIKERS
RIDE AGAIN

MICHAEL JOSEPH
an imprint of
PENGUIN BOOKS

DAVE: I would like to dedicate this book to my late Mam and Dad.
My father was a lifelong biker and I know he is with me when
I am on the bike, riding roads that he could only dream of.

SI: I would like to dedicate this book to my wife Jane for her
unwavering support, amazing insight and gentle words.

MICHAEL JOSEPH

Published by the Penguin Group

Penguin Books Ltd, 80 Strand, London WC2R 0RL, England

Penguin Group (USA) Inc., 375 Hudson Street, New York, New York 10014, USA

Penguin Group (Canada), 90 Eglinton Avenue East, Suite 700, Toronto, Ontario, Canada M4P 2Y3
(a division of Pearson Penguin Canada Inc.)

Penguin Ireland, 25 St Stephen's Green, Dublin 2, Ireland (a division of Penguin Books Ltd)

Penguin Group (Australia),
250 Camberwell Road,
Camberwell, Victoria 3124, Australia
(a division of Pearson Australia Group Pty Ltd)

Penguin Books India Pvt Ltd,
11 Community Centre, Panchsheel Park, New Delhi – 110 017, India

Penguin Group (NZ), 67 Apollo Drive, Rosedale, North Shore 0632,
New Zealand
(a division of Pearson New Zealand Ltd)

Penguin Books (South Africa) (Pty) Ltd, 24 Sturdee Avenue, Rosebank, Johannesburg 2196, South Africa

Penguin Books Ltd, Registered Offices: 80 Strand, London WC2R 0RL, England

www.penguin.com

First published 2007
1

Copyright © David Myers and Simon King, 2007

The moral rights of the authors have been asserted

Food photography © William Shaw, 2007

Jacket photography © Chris Terry

Reportage photography © Big Bear Films Ltd/VIXPIX Films Ltd and Chris Terry, 2007

Photographs taken on location by John Stroud, Vikram Jayanti, David Keene, Nicola Preston and Simon Weir

Stock library images by Alamy

Street scene (page 80, top right): Brian Atkinson / Alamy

Sign (page 87): Peter Adams Photography / Alamy

Maps © Dominic Trevett, 2007

By arrangement with the BBC
BBC logo copyright BBC 1996

The BBC logo is a registered trademark of the British Broadcasting Corporation and is used under licence.

The Hairy Bikers Ride Again is a Big Bear Films and VIXPIX Films co-production

Home economist: Sammy-Jo Squire

Props stylist: Sarah Waller

Designed by: Sarah Fraser and Sailesh Patel

Made and Printed in Italy
by Printer Trento, s.r.l.

A CIP catalogue record for this book is available from the British Library

INTRODUCTION

There are some rides where, as you swing your leg over the bike, you know to within a couple of minutes when you'll arrive at the other end. You know every pothole, every loose bit of scree on every dodgy bend and every pub car park to avoid at chucking-out time. Then there are other rides where, through error or instinct, you head off the well-worn track and suddenly every corner throws up a new surprise. The road less travelled swings through scenery that makes your jaw drop, amongst strangers who greet you like an old friend, and into smells and flavours that leave you drooling like a nutter. That's what the last year or so has been like for us.

From the first tentative steps on our journey, we've been hugely aware of how lucky we are. Our lifelong interest in food, bikes and travel has somehow struck a chord with an awful lot of people, and that shared enthusiasm has been the petrol in our engines from day one. It's not just been the hundreds of emails and letters, but also the friendly nod or thumbs up, often in the most unlikely of places. Dave found himself in a Bucharest bar while our Romania episode was showing on a TV in the corner. The response to it (and him) made it one of the proudest moments of his life.

The question we get asked most (even more than 'How the hell do you get away with talking bollocks for a living?') is 'How do you choose the places you visit?' Well, there's no straight answer. Both of us have a kind of mental wish list of countries and experiences that we've always wanted to try. Some of them get crossed off for practical reasons: cost, availability of bikes, some bird Kingy did a runner from who might still want to carve her initials on his back with an axe. And some are too close to what we all know: so let's do Portugal rather than Spain and let's do the Alentejo rather than the Algarve. In fact, what we try to do is choose places that are just on the edge of people's radar. Hence Namibia rather than South Africa, Romania not Rome and, this time round, Belgium rather than France, the mountains and deserts of Morocco rather than the beach resorts.

And what a collection of trips it's been. Four journeys, four continents and four astonishing experiences. We've washed elephants' bellies in Kerala and been out-bellied by elephant seals in Patagonia (and that takes some doing). We've taken part in a classic Indian ballet, a tango tea dance in Buenos Aires and a finch-twittering contest in Hulste. We've had sharks on our lines in the South Atlantic and snakes on our heads in Marrakech. And we've ridden through the rush hour in Chennai and lived . . .

But throughout it all, the most exciting discovery is always the food. The hardest part of the series, and the book, is trying to distil a thousand great eats into a handful of recipes. So we've gone for the dishes that we come back to time and again. These really are ones that you can warm your hands on – cracking recipes that don't take a lifetime to learn or a day to prepare, but which will leave you (and your mates) with that lovely warm glow that says 'proper food'. And in our opinion, there's no greater compliment than that.

Something we've always been aware of, but which our trips have constantly reinforced, is that wherever we've eaten, the best meals have always been those that seem to belong in the community that provides them. Whether celebrating the glories of an Argentinian steak in a Buenos Aires restaurant or singing and drumming round a simple table in Ouarzazate, it's that sense of unpretentious pride in the local produce that helps make a meal so memorable. So check out your local butcher, fishmonger, farmers' market – talk to them, ask their opinion, have a laugh with them. You'll be glad you did.

And don't forget: this book is written for you. It's not about you thinking we're dead clever, it's about us passing on some of the simple fun we've had over the past year.

Remember the motto: just give it a go . . .

Dave and Si

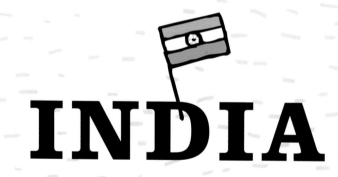

INDIA

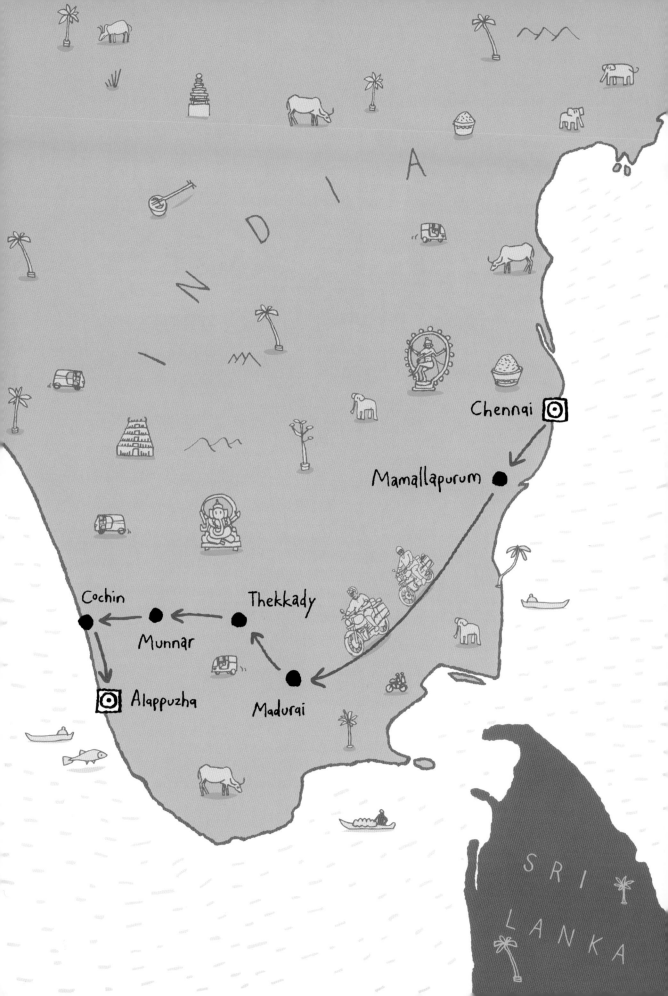

DAVE:

India, the great subcontinent. Ooh and yes, it ain't half hot mum. It's a huge country with a population of over a billion people and so big that, despite our Hairy Biker appetites and ambitions, we decided to limit ourselves to southern India. This is where we reckon the best food comes from.

The food culture in southern India is mostly vegetarian but food here lacks for nothing – it has variety, taste and texture. The cow is sacred, probably for economic reasons as much as spiritual ones. As cows supply milk, butter and manure for building work and fertilizer, it was decided a long time ago it would be a bit daft to eat them.

When I was a student, some twenty-five years ago, I tasted my first southern Indian food at the Sree Krishna restaurant in Tooting. It was a revelation. I even moved to Streatham to be closer to it. I lined the top box on my motorbike with polystyrene so I could get my curries and dosas home hot and I got myself a half-Indian girlfriend so the new lifestyle could be complete. She was a bit of a nutter, but that's another tale (she is, however, very happy now and has a thriving business making pickles. Sorry, I digress).

We decided to start our trip in Chennai, formerly known as Madras, because it's the home of the Royal Enfield factory. It was also the starting point for the British in India, so, like our forebears, we came and roasted. Chennai is always hot, but when we arrived in September it was hotter than a devil's slingback and clammier than a toad's T-shirt.

SI: Chennai is a strange city. The economic powerhouse of the south, it is in direct competition with Hyderabad and Delhi and they relish the fight. Everyone is busy, billboards advertise for staff to fill call centres and estate agents show off their latest acquisitions to foreign clients transported around in convoys of four-wheel drives. The new Indian economy is emerging so quickly that if you stand still long enough, you can see it in real time.

THE THALI

DAVE: Now, first things first. We wandered into a bustling shopping centre in Chennai and made our way to a food court in search of lunch. The usual stuff was there: Pizza Hut, noodle stands and coffee bars. But right in the middle was Sangeetha, a South Indian vegetarian restaurant, clearly thriving and very busy. Here we ordered a thali, the foundation of southern Indian veggie food.

The thali consisted of some twenty little dishes laid out on a banana leaf-lined tray (normally it's about twelve). The ingredients were ones that we would frequently encounter in the days to come. First there were the rasams and the sambars. The rasam, or pepper water, is hot and spicy, a thin gravy that is great if you have a cold. There might be a couple of different flavoured ones in a thali. The sambar is a thin, spicy vegetable curry. A couple of coconut chutneys are always included, set to one side of the tray and ready to be mixed into the rice as required. For sure, there will be a couple of dhals, a thin, split-pea type and a thick channa dhal made from chickpeas. Then there will also be some vegetable curries. In this case, there was an aloo gobi (a potato and cauliflower curry), a palak paneer (made from spinach and cheese), a bhindi bhaji (made from okra) and a mushroom curry.

> **'On the side was a big bowl of steamed rice and a blob of lime pickle sat angrily on the banana leaf.' DAVE**

A paratha was on top with a poppadom. The support band was a pot of curds to cool everything down. Lastly, there was a small bowl of tapioca dessert for pudding with a little banana on the side. Heavens. Oh, I nearly forgot, lurking somewhere under a dish or behind the bread was a paan, which is a betel leaf wrap containing betel nuts, aniseed, cloves and cardamom to cleanse your breath and settle your tum after this feast.

To eat the thali, you use your fingers to put a pile of rice in the middle of the banana leaf. Add the rasam, chutneys and sambar as you wish, then use the breads and your fingers as a vehicle to get the food to your mouth. It is the best, and all for the princely sum of just 90 rupees – little more than a pound.

THE ROYAL ENFIELD

DAVE: From here we went on to pick up our bikes. Enfield is a proper family firm and there are three generations of some families working on the production lines. It's industry like we used to have in Britain.

SI: The Enfields attracted us for several reasons, but largely because they are still built in the true tradition of motorcycling. If the bike breaks down, you can fix it without the aid of a computer and some diagnostic processing chip. All you need is a bit of savvy and some assorted tools – HURRAHHH!

The workers are proud of the product they produce and the work force rely on each other to maintain the quality of the bikes, albeit with materials that aren't cutting-edge in comparison with modern motorcycle manufacturers. So, if you want a bike with more history than Ben Hur and more character than Charlie Chaplin, then buy an Enfield from the lads in India because they deserve our support and admiration. **ALL POWER TO YOU BOYS**, long may it last.

DAVE: The works' canteen was one of the best bits. It was great food and one hundred per cent vegetarian. The workers could have vegetable biryanis, uppuma (a kind of savoury semolina porridge), thalis and all sorts of other treats. Once a week the workers get an egg in their biryani. The smell of all those spices, mixed with oil and petrol, was an intoxicating one. It reminded me a bit of Kingy.

SI: The bikes we secured from the lads were two European-spec 500cc single Machismos. Very kindly they had organized some hand-made hard panniers for us, mounted in a chrome cage to rival those to be found on the front end of a footballer's wife's 4x4. They were sturdy, heavy and durable, to say the least, but very welcome all the same.

It was time to get back through rush hour to the flat – a good hour's ride in heavy, heavy traffic to a part of the city called Adyar. The boys laughed as we left the factory and wished us luck. Did we need it!

'So, if you want a bike with more history than Ben Hur and more character than Charlie Chaplin, then buy an Enfield from the lads in India.' SI

Now, if you ever get the opportunity to ride in India, you MUST, MUST do it! It really is a fantastic buzz and rush. However, you will need all the skill and courage you can muster, vigorously blended with bucket loads of luck and a generous sprinkling of divine intervention.

The Indians drive on the same side of the road as we do. Well, to be more precise, they drive on whatever side of the road takes their fancy, so don't be lulled into a false sense of security. At first, being in the traffic feels quite intimidating, but you do soon realize that the speed everyone is doing is quite low, other than the buses and long-distance haulage wagons who are, without doubt, kings of the road. You can tell when one is near because the horn they sound is as deep and as loud as the QE2 and they simply will not stop for God, Shiva or Gandhi. Many of these drivers have driven for days on bad roads, so it's best to pull over and give them a wide berth – you have been warned!

In the city, all bets are off and everyone just goes for it. There is no lane discipline and, oh God, THE HORNS. You must understand that anything with wheels has a horn and it is used constantly to tell fellow road-users that you're overtaking, undertaking, behind, in front, alongside on the left, alongside on the right or that you're going for a gap in the traffic that has yet to appear. It's sounded to say good morning, good evening, how's ya granny and fifth cousin twice-removed? Did your sister get the sari she was after? What did you have for lunch? It's a language all of its own. Add to all this two big Europeans and a happy local population trying to say hello and welcome to India through their car window or ox cart while moving ever closer to your front wheel and you start to get an idea of the chaos that abounds – WE LOVED IT!

THE BUTTERBALL

DAVE: The time had come to get out of the city. The bikes ran like a dream, but Chennai was hard and, with the body fed, it was time to feed the soul. We decided to head south out of Chennai, our potato exhausts popping away. Our route south was down the infamous ECR (East Coast Road) to a world heritage site called Mamallapuram.

Riding along the ECR you see how this coast was savaged by the tsunami. When you spot a waterline up to the third storey of a tower block, half a mile from the beach, you begin to realize how hellish and vast the tsunami was. You also get a real sense of the scale of the tragedy that somehow didn't come over on the news. A chill went down my spine as I looked out at the calm sea and the fishermen going about their business, much as they had done that Christmas a couple of years ago.

Our destination, Mamallapuram, started out as a big mound of boulders on the Bay of Bengal. Before long, artists arrived and started to chisel and, over a period of about fifteen hundred years, the boulders were carried off and used to build shrines. We went at dawn to the shore temple, probably the oldest stone temple in South India. As we watched the sunrise, the light lifted our senses and our spirits. This is a special place, surviving over a millennium – and the tsunami. Now it was time to get down to business. We were here to cook and we wanted to do this underneath Krishna's butterball.

'We went at dawn to the shore temple, probably the oldest stone temple in South India. As we watched the sunrise, the light lifted our senses and our spirits.' DAVE

Krishna's butterball is a massive boulder, as big as a block of flats, which appears to be balanced precariously on the edge of a hill. The story is that Lord Krishna, who loved butter, made a giant ball out of the creamy spread that was turned into stone. We were drawn to this site by its Raiders of the Lost Ark kind of vibe and because it's a holy site. So, we decided to cook a vegetarian meal.

'Now in this game, I bet you think we turn up in a limo, get out, pick the best produce, talk bollocks and get a big, fat paycheck. It isn't like that . . . well, perhaps the talking bollocks bit is.' DAVE

Now in this game, I bet you think we turn up in a limo, get out, pick the best produce, talk bollocks and get a big, fat paycheck. It isn't like that . . . well, perhaps the talking bollocks bit is. This was a cookery day that went totally wrong. Two weeks earlier we had gone to see the site and thought it would be a really cool place to cook. So our fixers applied to everyone from the government in Delhi to the local ice-cream man to try and get permission. All seemed well.

The food bit was easy. We were going to make stuffed parathas and palak paneer (a cheese and spinach curry). We would serve this with a raita and coconut chutney. Then, Si and I started getting creative. We thought it would be fun to have musicians, Bollywood dancers, ice-cream sellers and a masseuse on set, all rounded off with a yogi sitting on a table tied in a knot. You know, just a regular day at the office.

When we arrived at the site, all the tables were set up, flowers were everywhere and big sculptures started to appear of Ganesh, the

elephant god, Shivas and Krishnas. It was like one of George Harrison's psychedelic dreams. This all boded well – it was going to be the best shot yet. The Bollywood dancers arrived, the musicians came and the yogi turned up (this man could cut his hair with his feet. As they say, he was a regular top turn). Now down to business.

Full of pride we began our introduction. Looking up at Krishna's butterball Kingy cried:

'Here we are – you don't get this in Shields.'

'Ah, but we've got balls as big as this in Barrow!'

That's it! We were off. But not for long. A slight, diminutive man appeared in a cardie, big glasses balanced on the end of his nose. 'STOP!' he cried and, since he had two men in uniform behind him armed with riot sticks and self-loading rifles, we did just that.

'Do you have permission for the statues and the flowers?'

'Nah,' replied Kingy, 'who are you, the statue and flower police?'

Well, it turned out this man was.

So with two bare tables we started again. But things went from bad to worse. We had to stop until the Head of Flower and Statue Police had spoken to his superiors. Two hours later, we were still waiting. No dancing was allowed and as for music, forget it. The yogi had to untangle himself and went home. Undaunted, we cracked on and made the stuffed parathas, but then Mr Killjoy appeared again. We had to stop cooking until we paid him a fee for a permit. Well, we don't have money to burn so we packed up and told him to stuff it.

THE TEMPLE

SI: Back to the digs and we prepared for a ten-hour ride south to the temple city of Madurai. This road trip was the longest leg we had to ride, but we were determined to get there in a day so we could spend the following day in the famous temple complex of Sri Meenakshi. The journey went well as the bikes thumped their way through the ever-changing countryside (what a joy they were to ride). We also made time to stop at a couple of roadside stalls for chai and deep-fried loveliness.

DAVE: Indian tea is very strong, sweet and milky, but so refreshing. People sit around and really talk over their tea. It's a bit like going to the pub, but without the beer. Sweets are available too, treats like coconut ice and gulab jamuns (fried syrup balls), which are just the thing to restore the dusty traveller.

Sri Meenakshi is one of the wonders of the world, a beautiful, mad, baroque extravaganza of a building. We went on a Friday, a holy day when around 25,000 faithful come to worship. To be part of this was one of the most powerful experiences of my life.

When we rode up to the temple we were met by a sight that stopped us in our tracks. First we heard drums, then we saw the parade of penitents, men with twelve-foot javelins stuck through their cheeks, their skin pierced by butchers' hooks. In their trance-like state, they felt no pain. We could not believe what we were seeing. On our way into the temple, we placed some coins in the temple elephant's trunk and waited for him to tap us on the head as a blessing.

SI: Now, I have a theory about temple elephants. As I was waiting to be blessed, I took note that the more money you gave the ellie, the gentler the blessing. The only problem was I had just a five rupee coin. True to form, the blessing from said trunk was more like a Glasgow kiss.

DAVE: Inside the temple, the smell of incense and jasmine flowers was overwhelming; it's a bit like being on the set of a blockbuster film. A Brahman took my hand and guided my prayers as I prostrated myself before the altar. I was just then filled with an overwhelming sense of love. I looked at Si. We both had garlands of flowers wrapped around our necks, blobs of colour on our heads and white powder from Ganesh in lines on our foreheads. Si looked blissed out. This was a very special day.

On our way out, the Brahman gave us a little parcel of hot food that had been blessed, urging us to eat. It was the food of the gods. Si and I sat in the sunshine savouring a very rich, spicy and sweet rice pudding. What a great religion. Kids run screaming into the temple to bang a bell, you leave full of love, your spirit lifted and, importantly for us, your belly full.

THE SPICE GIRLS

SI: All at one with the universe, Dave and I set off for the Cardamom Hills and the spice plantations that surround Kumily and Thekkady. The plains gave way to the mountains and the air started to get cooler and cleaner. Oh deep joy, a chance to stop sweating for a bit.

It's an interesting time when you first ride into a town because it's always mayhem. Having ridden on relatively quiet roads, you hit a town and all hell breaks loose. Cars, trucks, autorickshaws and those sacred cows wander the town in a sort of mad recipe of wandering ingredients, all ready to be placed on the gods' large stove, boiled and served up as a road traffic accident. It's always a time of intense concentration for Dave and I. Arriving in Kumily, though, we were distracted by the wonderful smell of spices being sold in the shops on either side of the main road.

DAVE: Spices are very important in Ayurvedic medicine and so it's no coincidence that some of the spice shops in Kumily resemble pharmacies. Ayurveda is a holistic way of life, and food, which is seen as medicinal, is part of this. Spices are nearly always used for their healing powers as well

as for their taste. For instance, cardamom is used as a digestive and is meant to cool the blood, while cloves soothe an aching tooth. Turmeric is probably the most important spice, used as an antiseptic, for a sore throat or to smooth the skin and discourage hair growth (you end up with perfect skin, but the turmeric colours you as yellow as a corn-fed chicken).

It was in Kumily that we met the spice girls. Smelling the cardamoms from two hundred metres away, we walked into a cardamom merchant's office in which sat about thirty beautiful, sari-clad ladies. The gossip stopped as we came near. Somebody said something and then the place collapsed in laughter. Umm, they were probably thinking how handsome we were?

SI: The ladies sit in teams at the warehouse, sifting through the cardamoms. The crack is thick and fast, but was completely incomprehensible to us because it was in Tamil. But when you talk to as many people as Dave and I do, you develop a sixth sense of what is being said:

'Have you seen these two big white lads, Davindra, I wonder what they're after?'

'Well, you never know with those sort of folk. Oh, hold on a minute, one of them has a film camera.'

'Quick, quick, adjust your sari and smile. Fill your basket and look busy.'

'The things these lot find interesting is beyond me.'

'They're two funny-looking fellas, aren't they?'

'Well, they all look the same to me.'

DAVE: So we smiled, said goodbye and scarpered, slightly red in the cheeks. With our panniers full of delicious cardamoms, we headed through to Thekkady, where on the veranda of a Maharaja's summer hunting lodge, we cooked king prawn pakoras and palak paneer and created what is quite simply one of the best dry martinis ever made. In the old days, people would come here to shoot tigers; now this place exists to preserve them. It reeked of history.

TIFFIN AT THE
HIGH RANGE CLUB

SI: The following morning we were to leave for Munnar, a place famous for its tea plantations. It was only a 110km ride, but the trip would take us a good four hours because the road was narrow, winding and dotted with potholes. Any loss of concentration on this route and the potential to end up as a messy decoration on the front of a bus was only too real. In addition, Dave had recently recovered from an accident and was managing, mile by mile, to ride his way back to confident and competent riding with remarkable fortitude. Riding in India is a baptism of fire and I must say my mate has more bottle than your local dairy.

As we rode, the spice fields gave way to terraces of tea and the mountains became larger and more striking. The delay in our arrival in Munnar wasn't really the road, but the unbelievably beautiful views. We could not help but stop and take in as much of the scenery as we could. It got to the point of complete overload. It was a fantastic ride and must go down as one of our best runs.

On arrival in Munnar, we passed women loaded with baskets of tea strapped to their heads, toiling up steep terraces of tea bushes that would have been difficult for a mountain goat. The wicker baskets were left on the roadside to await

'**Tiffin is a generic term for a snack. However, the British used the term to refer to teatime: 'Whoopee, memsahib, it's five o'clock and time for tiffin.'** DAVE

collection, so Dave and I pulled the bikes over and decided to try and lift a couple to test the weight. Bloody hell! It nearly put our backs out, much to the amusement of the tea pickers who had gathered to witness two big lads grunting and groaning.

DAVE: The first tea planters in this area came from Scotland around 1900. You can see how this area reminded the planters of home; it's cool, with highlands and waterfalls. India is today one of the world's great tea growers, but commercial tea planting was only started in the twentieth century by the British.

SI: We needed to get to our digs and in Munnar this meant the High Range Club, a place that had been a club for the officers and gentlemen of the Raj.

DAVE: This was a hoot. A true relic from India's colonial past, the High Range Club was the social hub for the planters. Today the club is shabby and the tennis courts decrepit, but this little corner of the Empire still survives, albeit now as a club run by Indians for Indians.

The old traditions and dress codes are still observed. We were met by the manager, who we immediately named Basil Fawlty. He took one look at us and decided he didn't like what he saw. The crew in their sandals and shorts weren't up to his standards and we were informed that no alcohol was allowed after ten o'clock. Oh no, and it was our day off tomorrow!

We headed straight for the main bar. Pith helmets were nailed to the wall with the names of the old hunters painted on them, moth-eaten tiger heads arranged next door. Rugger and cricket team portraits were hung everywhere, with descriptions like 'The High Range Club versus Cochin First Fifteen, 1926'. This was a glimpse into another world and time and it was the appropriate place to cook tiffin. Tiffin on the terrace – can't say that when you're pissed.

Tiffin is a generic term for a snack. There are tiffin stalls on every street corner selling vadas (lentil doughnuts), pakoras and all sorts of treats. However, the British used the term to refer to teatime: 'Whoopee, memsahib, it's five o'clock and time for tiffin.'

So we cooked our version of vadas, which were delicious dipped into a fruity coconut chutney. We also made shrikhand, a traditional pudding, which we layered over fruit (see the recipe). As we ate our tiffin washed down with chai and served by liveried waiters, we began to see just how seductive this lifestyle must have been.

THE LAND OF THE COCONUT

SI: Leaving Munnar, we headed west towards the Keralan coast and Cochin. We were desperate for a nice bit of fish. Ooh, the place did not disappoint.

DAVE: We arrived on the west coast with a sense of satisfaction that we had now ridden right across India. Kerala is like heaven on Earth. 'Kera' means coconut and 'la' means land. We had arrived in the land of the coconut.

We set off to buy some fish, and what a fish market it was. One item that often gets overlooked in Indian food is seafood, but the fish, especially in Kerala and

Goa, are number one. There were varieties we had never seen and prawns the size of whippets. We bought a really fresh kingfish as fresh and solid as a Geordie girl on a big night out. The food here is very different from the creamy Moghul kitchen. You have very dry curries called thorans, which are spicy, crunchy and flavoured with coconut, as well as the thinner-than-a-thin-thing rasams.

Clasping our fishy feast we rode down to Alappuzha, supposedly the Venice of India, with its labyrinth of canals and bridges. On a Keralan houseboat we cooked a dry masala fish curry with our kingfish. To go with this, we made a tomato and coconut chutney. This was our take on Keralan food and if you're only going to try one dish in the book, make it this one.

'Leaving Munnar, we headed west towards the Keralan coast and Cochin. We were desperate for a nice bit of fish. Ooh, the place did not disappoint.' SI

We were soon joined by a sitar and tabla player and we have to confess that, after we finished filming, we set sail for an hour, drifting as the sun went down through the creeks and canals of Alappuzha. Perks of the job, mate!

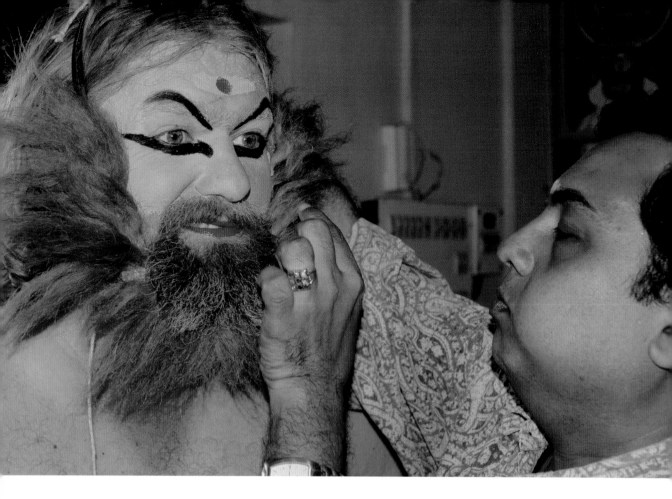

KATHAKALI

DAVE: The next day was one of the maddest we have ever had, and we have had some nutty ones. We visited a Kathakali theatre and, with a bit of blagging, we became part of the play. Kathakali is a unique form of ritualized theatre. Well, that's the posh explanation. I would describe it as a highly sophisticated version of pantomime crossed with morris dancing.

Our first stop was the make-up room. Si was to be a Brahman, a holy man and leader (well, it made him happy!). I was to be Karutha Thaadi, a garishly painted hunter wearing the biggest tutu you have ever seen (well, that made me happy!). You may or may not know, but I worked for about twenty years doing make-up for films and telly. This was very different. Firstly, you strip off to your underpants and lie flat on your back on the floor. The make-up master then straddled me and started to paint me black . . . and I mean paint. Afterwards he built up my chops with a kind of Polyfilla.

I collapsed in giggles when I caught sight of Kingy. He was a delicate shade of peach, wearing more eye make-up than a Blackpool landlady on a night out and his goatee beard was crafted into a monster.

SI: Make-up finished, I looked at myself in the mirror. Seconds before, Dave had told me that I was the same colour as his Aunty Mabel's bathroom suite – a vision in peach. And true to form, he was right. I had red lips, my face was peach and my false beard had encompassed my real one perfectly. But I actually thought to myself, I quite fancy me in a strange sort of way (don't tell anyone I told you that, OK?).

DAVE: Next, the costumes came out. Kingy, keeping up the Blackpool landlady theme, wore a kaftan-type robe; you know, the sort fat girls wear. Mine was a monster tutu. Does my bum look big in this? Yeah, Myers, truly massive.

'I collapsed in giggles when I caught sight of Kingy. He was a delicate shade of peach, wearing more eye make-up than a Blackpool landlady.' DAVE

SI: The other actors showed us a couple of hand movements and Dave and I were lulled into thinking, great, all we have to do is move our hands in that sort of Bollywood way and we're laughing. OHHHHHH NOOOOO. The lads with the drums kicked off the dancing nice and slow, then it just got faster and louder and faster and louder until we began to sweat and bits started to fall off our costumes.

DAVE: We did try hard to follow the balletic movements, but we still ended up looking like drunken turkeys. The Kathakali men are not just actors, they are athletes with a great spiritual belief behind them. What an amazing glimpse into another world; long may it thrive.

SUNITA

DAVE: Before we went home, Si fixed up a last treat for me. One morning, after a dawn dander through the forest, Si pulled us into a school that trained elephants for work in the forests, temples and in construction. It was there that I fell in love. She was called Sunita, just like the gorgeous lass from Coronation Street. She was 36 years old, just like her, and she had massive brown eyes, just like her. But there the similarities ended. This Sunita was grey and wrinkly and weighed four tonnes.

I took her to the river (well, like I was able to stop her). We jumped in and, in an act of love, she let me wash her and scrub behind her ears. I hit the magic spot, her eyes rolled and she lashed out with her trunk – nearly taking my head off in the process. Elephants are magic. Here, the mahouts who look after them have a very close bond with their charges because the elephants need love or they go mad, get ill and refuse to work (a bit like Si). I left the river with Sunita and walked off into a new day.

You soon get used to India being a bit dirty and chaotic, and when you smile at someone in India, you get a genuine smile back. You eat the best food in the world and there is an amazing spiritual depth that we were both touched by. India is magnificent and I can't wait to go back. So be kind to yourself, go and visit while the old India is still around. Better still, do it on a Royal Enfield.

THE FOOD

DAVE: Indian food: yum, yum, my favourite. In fact, we are a nation of addicts because it's a medical truth that when a curry addict thinks of curry or a night at their local tandoori, the same chemicals are released in the brain that fuel a drug addict's craving. But Indian food is much more than tandoori chicken tikka masala, pulao rice and a stuffed naan down the curry house, it's an ever evolving, vibrant combination of tastes.

In the South, a lot of the people are vegetarian and over the years they have developed a very sophisticated and refined cuisine. This is vegetarian food a million miles away from rainbow jumpers and the worthy rissoles some vegetarian cafés at home dish up. The vegetarian cooking of India has its textures and flavours properly worked out and YOU WILL NOT MISS MEAT. In the time we were in India, we both went veggie and found we felt great and lost a few pounds too.

THE PICKLE TRAY

Chutneys and raita are your Indian condiments and they put our salt and pepper to shame. Forget the festering chrome salmonella trolley in your local tandoori, a good pickle tray provides you with an artist's palette of tastes. You have sweet mango chutney, which goes with everything, and to temper this, sharp, hot lime pickle. You have chilli pickles and my favourite brinjal pickle, made from aubergines and rich and flavoursome (great with a cheese sandwich by the way). On its way to being a raita is the dish of raw onions and tomatoes, which cools and gives a bit of crunch. Raita, made from cucumber, mint and yoghurt, is made to chill out an angry vindaloo.

'Chutneys and raita are your Indian condiments and they put our salt and pepper to shame.' DAVE

RICE

In the North, people tend to eat breads like chapatis and naan with their curries, but down South, rice is all the rage, with basmati and patna being the most popular (my favourite, though, is Keralan rice, with grains the size of fat maggots, just perfect to absorb the South's saucy curries).

And rice never has to be plain. Fry it first in a little oil, and then boil with some whole spices like cardamoms and cinnamon to make a pulao rice. Stick in a few peas and that's a peas pulao. Stir in mustard seeds, lemon zest, lemon leaves and juice to make a lemon rice (great with fish). Or grate in coconut and add coconut milk to make a coconut rice to go with chicken or meat. You can add mixed vegetable or even mushrooms.

Sometimes the rice and the curry get cooked together in a one-pot wonder. This is a biryani. You layer the rice with the curry, dabble on yoghurt, dot with saffron and bake it all together. The flavours are ace.

DHAL

Pulses, or dhal, play a big part in Indian cookery. They are a high-protein staple that can be used as a main or a side dish. Chickpeas or channa dhal are as common here as in Middle Eastern food. The chickpeas can also be ground into gram flour, and it is this that is used in pakoras. Urad dhal are small, delicate lentils that need no soaking and are often cooked with rice. Masoor dhal are good old-fashioned red lentils and toor dhal are like our split peas. Indian cuisine also uses dried mung beans, dried peas and butter beans.

OUR TOP TEN SPICES

DAVE: This brings us to spices. We thought we'd compile a top ten of the most popular ones and how to use them.

10 Fennel seeds Their taste is warm and mellow with an undertone of aniseed. Lovely with vegetables.

9 Asafoetida Not very well known, but a personal favourite. It comes in little yellow pots and is a yellow powder that just stinks. It contains sulphur and smells of rotten eggs, but trust me, put a pinch of this in your curry and it gives it a lovely finish.

8 Cloves Very, very strong and sharp in flavour, use sparingly in stocks and rice.

7 Saffron More expensive than gold. The stigma of a crocus, three-quarters of a million flowers yield only 1lb saffron. It has a unique taste so use it sparingly, but it is great with rice or chicken.

6 Cardamom My favourite spice (do please try our cardamom chicken recipe, it's fabulous). The best are the green cardamoms. You need to give the seed pods a bash to release their flavour or extract the seeds and crush them in a pestle and mortar before use.

5 Cumin (jeera) Very distinctive and great with lamb. It has a warm taste and is a bit bitter.

4 Cinnamon Use the bark whole or in a powdered form. The taste is warm, sweet and aromatic. Great with puddings, but also works well with cloves in spice blends.

3 Mustard seeds The seeds are either black or white and are great when fried first to get them to pop and release their lovely aroma. Brilliant with potatoes.

2 Turmeric An important one and the heart and soul of many curries. It gives an earthy taste to food and will send everything a wonderful golden colour (this includes your worktops and false teeth).

1 Coriander The leaf, seeds and root are all used. Like it or loathe it, it's one of the most important spices and gives a distinctive flavour.

This is just the tip of the iceberg, so go to your local Asian shop, explore, make friends and find more wonderful spices (very often the vegetables in Asian grocers are fresher and cheaper than those in the supermarkets too).

'We British just love our Indian curries. They are now more popular than fish and chips...'

DAVE

THE BRITISH CURRY

We British just love our Indian curries. They are now more popular than fish and chips. The first Indian restaurant in Britain was opened almost two hundred years ago in Portman Square by one Dean Mahomed. The restaurant was called The Hindoostane Coffee House and there wasn't a roll of flock wallpaper in sight (by the way, the flock wallpaper wasn't a style thing; it was used because it was cheap and rapidly going out of fashion in the seventies).

The Hindoostane Coffee House was a real classy joint and even the Times announced that it cooked 'Indian dishes in the highest perfection . . . unequalled to any curries ever made in England, with choice wines'.

But like a lot of curry joints, it went bust within three years. Later, Queen Victoria, who had a number of Indian servants, could frequently be heard screaming around the corridors of Buckingham Palace that she could murder an Indian. She was also quite partial to a curry. The first proper Indian restaurant came in the shape of Veeraswamy's, which opened in 1926 just off Piccadilly. The food won rave reviews and the place was soon chic and popular and patronized by royalty.

In 1955 there were still only nine Indian restaurants in London and four in the provinces, though there were humble cafés down by the docks pushing out curry and rice for Indian sailors in return for a couple of pennies. But by the late sixties and the seventies, there had been an explosion of Indian food and those Vestas were all the rage. In Barrow-in-Furness at the age of fourteen, I was listening to Jethro Tull and pouring boiling water onto what looked like spicy sawdust. I felt very sophisticated savouring my Vesta beef curry. Indian restaurants opened by the dozen. As Madhur Jaffrey said, it was 'an ironic example of reverse colonization!'

Ooh, this is making me hungry. Ta, ta, I'm off for a curry!

LAMB CHOP PAKORAS   SERVES 4

These taste heavenly with the spicy, crisp coating giving way to a lamb pasanda flavour all on a little handle. Ask your butcher to 'French trim' the chops, which means to scrape the fat off the bones to make clean handles.

for the batter
100g gram (or plain) flour
1 teaspoon black mustard seeds
100ml thick natural yoghurt
1 teaspoon salt
½ teaspoon cayenne pepper

1kg lamb chops or cutlets,
 French trimmed
1 teaspoon cumin seeds
1 teaspoon coriander seeds
1 teaspoon black peppercorns

750ml milk
1 cinnamon stick
2 green chillies, thinly sliced
5 cloves
12 cardamom pods, bruised
 (i.e. gently bashed with a rolling
 pin or in a pestle and mortar)
a thumb-sized piece of ginger, grated
1 onion, finely chopped
vegetable oil, for deep-frying
sea salt and lime wedges, to serve

If your lovely butcher hasn't already done it, trim the lamb chops of fat and scrape the bones clean (these will become handles to eat the nuggets of gorgeousness).

In a dry frying pan, dry roast the cumin and coriander seeds for a minute, place in a pestle and mortar with the peppercorns and grind finely.

Pour the milk into a heavy saucepan and add the cinnamon, chilli, cloves, cardamom seeds, ginger and onion. Bring to the boil and bung in your chops. Turn off the heat and let them sit in the hot milk mixture, making sure they are fully covered, then add the lid. After 5 minutes, turn them over and repeat for another 5 minutes. Blot dry.

While this is happening, make a batter: put the gram flour, mustard seeds, yoghurt, 1 tablespoon water, salt and cayenne pepper in a mixing bowl and beat together until they form a thick paste, adding more water, a little at a time, if necessary. The batter should be thick enough to give your chops a good coating.

Heat enough oil to completely cover the chops in a heavy pan until it is very, very hot. Dip the chops in the batter, keeping the bones clear so they can become little handles. Fry for about 2 minutes until golden. Let them rest for 5 minutes before serving. Serve the pakoras with flakes of sea salt and lime quarters. A little raita on the side is a good thing too.

KING PRAWN PAKORAS

MAKES ABOUT 20–25 PAKORAS AND FEEDS 4 HUNGRY MEN

Freshly cooked pakoras are a real luxury. The batter is prepared with gram flour (also called besan flour), which is made from chickpeas. A nice touch is to add spices, especially mustard seeds, to the batter because the seeds release their flavour as the pakoras fry.

We've kept these very simple, so you get just the king prawns in a spicy, crunchy coating.

for the batter
140g gram (or plain) flour
1 teaspoon black mustard seeds
110ml natural yoghurt
1 green chilli,
  seeded and finely chopped
3 spring onions, finely chopped
zest of ½ lime
1 teaspoon salt

400g raw king prawns
a sprinkle of salt
vegetable oil, for deep-frying
lemon wedges, to serve

Wash the prawns and blot dry on a piece of kitchen roll. Sprinkle with salt.

Heat the oil in a pan or deep-fat fryer to approximately 160°C.

In the meantime, combine all the batter ingredients in a bowl with 75ml water. Dip the prawns into the batter and shake off the excess, while keeping a good coating.

Cook the pakoras gently in the oil for about 5 minutes until they are golden and the prawns are cooked all the way through.

Serve with lemon wedges and perhaps a raita. These are also brilliant with sweet chilli sauce (a bottled supermarket one will do).

ANDREW'S SAMBAR   SERVES 4–6

Andrew is a top bloke we met while staying in Chennai. We got chatting about food at a chai stop on the street, found out he was a keen cook and picked his brains for some recipes. This is his version of the southern Indian staple sambar. It's the southern Indian equivalent of gravy and is usually served with rice.

for the dhal
1 red onion, chopped
3 tomatoes, reserve 2 and chop 1
2 cloves of garlic, peeled
100g toor dhal
4 shallots, quartered
½ teaspoon turmeric
½ teaspoon salt

2 tablespoons vegetable oil
½ teaspoon black mustard seeds
½ teaspoon fenugreek seeds

1 teaspoon cumin seeds
1 small dried red chilli
1 whole green chilli
10 curry leaves
½ teaspoon asafoetida
½ teaspoon turmeric
1 teaspoon ground coriander
1 teaspoon chilli powder
1 aubergine, cut into 2–3cm cubes
1 potato, cut into 2–3cm cubes
2 teaspoons tamarind paste
1 teaspoon chopped fresh coriander
1 teaspoon ghee (or vegetable oil)

Put half the red onion, the chopped tomato and both the garlic cloves in a medium-sized saucepan. Add the dhal, shallots, turmeric and salt. Cover with 750ml water, bring to the boil and simmer for 20 minutes. When the dhal is soft, gently mash the mixture. Set aside.

Pour the oil into another saucepan. When the oil is hot, add the mustard seeds. Wait until they pop, then add the fenugreek seeds, cumin seeds, dried red chilli, fresh green chilli and curry leaves and fry for a minute.

Chop the remaining two tomatoes and add with the other half of the onion. Sprinkle in the asafoetida, turmeric, ground coriander and chilli powder and cook for a further minute.

Add the aubergine and potato and cook for 8 minutes, putting in a couple of tablespoons of water so as not to burn the ingredients.

Now add the dhal mix to the pan with the aubergine and cook for 5 minutes, seasoning to taste.

Mix the tamarind paste with 100ml water and pour this into the pan, cooking for a further 3 minutes or so. Finally, add the fresh coriander and ghee, stir and serve.

VEGETABLE SAMOSAS   MAKES 10–12

There is nothing better than a home-made samosa, so far removed is it from those petrol-station disasters. In fact, our programme owes a lot to samosas. Years ago, we were on a train in India and a character came on selling wonderful hot samosas that cost pennies. We started talking with him about his life on the trains and his wife, who cooked the samosas and bhajis, and we thought wouldn't it be great to visit his house, get the recipe and have a crack with the wife and kids? This has been the essence of our programme ever since.

Don't be put off by having to make the pastry yourself – it's really easy.

for the pastry
250g plain flour
1 teaspoon salt
2 teaspoons vegetable oil
1 egg, separated

for the filling
2 potatoes, peeled
2 large carrots, very finely chopped
2 tablespoons vegetable oil
1 small onion, very finely chopped
½ teaspoon turmeric
2 teaspoons garam masala

1 teaspoon black mustard seeds
1 teaspoon salt
½ teaspoon ground black pepper
4 cloves of garlic, crushed
1 green chilli, chopped
  (or half if you don't like it hot!)
10 curry leaves
75g frozen peas
1 teaspoon lemon juice
a handful of chopped
  coriander leaves

vegetable oil, for deep-frying

First make the pastry by placing the flour and salt in a bowl and working in the oil and egg yolk until the flour becomes crumblike. Pour in up to 135ml warm (blood temperature) water, a little at a time, and mix until you get a stiff, elastic dough. Chill the dough ball in the refrigerator while you make the filling.

Cook the potatoes whole in a pan of boiling water for about 15 minutes or until tender. Lift out of the pan, reserving the water, and set aside to cool. When cool, chop finely.

In the boiling potato water, cook the carrots for just 2 minutes. Drain and set aside.

Add the oil to a frying pan and, when hot, sweat the onion (cook it over a low heat) until soft but not brown. Add the turmeric, garam masala, mustard seeds, salt and pepper and cook for a minute, then add the garlic and chilli and toss together for 2 minutes. Scatter the curry leaves into the pan and cook for a further minute. Add the potato and carrot and mix gently but thoroughly into the spices.

Cook over a low heat for a further 10 minutes to release all the flavours into the potato. Add the peas and cook gently for a further 2 to 3 minutes. Finally, add the lemon juice and coriander and season. Leave to go cold.

To assemble your samosas, roll out your pastry not too thin, not too thick (about 3mm), then take a small side plate and make an impression in the pastry. Cut round this with a knife, then cut the round in half and form each half into a cone, with the edges of the cone overlapping. Use your fingers to squash the two edges gently together to seal. Your cones are now ready for the filling.

Spoon the filling into the cones until three-quarters full (do not overfill). Brush the top edge with the egg white and seal the filling into the cone, using your fingers to pinch the top edge together. Repeat with the rest of the pastry and filling.

Heat the oil in a pan or deep-fat fryer to approximately 180°C or until it is very hot and gently rumbling, and deep-fry the samosas for about 5 minutes until golden and crunchy. These are very good served with some chutney and raita.

STUFFED PARATHAS   MAKES 6

This is my favourite Indian bread . . . and yes, it probably is the most fattening, but by crikey it's tasty.

4 potatoes

400g plain flour

½ teaspoon baking powder

1 teaspoon sugar

1 teaspoon salt

1 egg

220ml milk

1 tablespoon vegetable oil

a thumb-sized piece of ginger, finely chopped

1 onion, chopped extra fine

2 cloves of garlic, finely chopped

2 green chillies, finely chopped

½ teaspoon turmeric

1 teaspoon chilli powder

1 teaspoon ground coriander

1 teaspoon garam masala

2 tablespoons finely chopped fresh coriander

4–5 tablespoons ghee (or vegetable oil)

First, peel the potatoes and cut them into small chunks. Then put them in a pan of cold water and bring to the boil. When the potatoes are cooked (after about 25 minutes), mash them and set aside.

In a mixing bowl, mix the flour, baking powder, sugar and salt together with the egg and milk to make a dough. Slap it around and beat the living daylights out of it for about ten minutes. Cover with clingfilm and leave it to rest for 15 minutes.

In a frying pan, heat the oil and add the ginger, onion, garlic and chillies. Fry for a couple of minutes until soft. Add the turmeric, chilli powder, ground coriander and garam masala. Cook for another 2 minutes.

Mix the mashed potatoes into the onion spice mix. Taste and add salt to adjust the seasoning. Finally mix in the coriander. Divide the potato mixture into six, roll into balls and set aside.

Divide the dough into six balls. Flour the kitchen worktop and roll the dough balls into discs about 1½cm thick. Place a ball of the potato filling in the middle of each disc and bring the edges up around the filling so it looks like a giant dim sum dumpling. Twist the top to seal it. Turn the ball-shaped paratha over and, with a bit of flour sprinkled on the top to stop everything sticking together, roll very gently into a flat disc.

Coat a flat frying pan with ghee and heat until very hot. Place the parathas messy-side down and leave for a couple of minutes to cook. Brush a layer of ghee on the top side and then flip and cook for another couple of minutes until golden.

CHAPATIS MAKES 10

Chapatis, or rotis, are the everyday bread of India and home-baked bread is always best. They are really simple to cook, so when your mates are round for a curry, knock up some home-made chapatis and make it a bit special.

250g wholemeal flour
½ teaspoon salt
1 tablespoon vegetable oil

Sift the flour into a large mixing bowl and add the salt.

Work in the oil to make the flour crumblike, then add up to 120ml cold water, bit by bit, to create a medium-soft dough. Now you need to knead it for about 10 minutes, working it and loving it like James Brown working an audience.

Roll the dough into a sausage shape and cut into 10 equal slices. Leave to rest for 10 minutes. Then, on a floured surface, roll the slices into thin discs like pancakes.

In a hot dry pan, cook the chapatis on both sides for about a minute until golden. As they puff up, press them down on the pan with a spatula to get them to catch and form tasty burnt bits.

GOLL BHAJI   MAKES 12 OR SO BHAJIS

A great dish to serve with drinks before dinner. In the days of the Raj, this little snack would have been part of an assortment of afternoon treats called tiffin, a generic name for any snack served in between meals. So go on, have a bit of tiffin.

75g cashew nuts
1 teaspoon fennel seeds
100g rice flour
100g gram (or plain) flour
½ teaspoon bicarbonate of soda
1 teaspoon salt
½ teaspoon ground black pepper
½ teaspoon chilli powder
a thumb-sized piece of ginger, chopped

1 tablespoon finely chopped fresh coriander
1 onion, finely chopped
1 tablespoon ghee (or vegetable oil)
1 small egg, beaten
vegetable oil, for deep-frying
lime wedges, to serve

In a dry frying pan, dry roast the cashew nuts and fennel seeds until the cashews have taken some colour, then chop finely.

In a mixing bowl, combine the rice flour, gram flour, bicarbonate of soda, salt and pepper.

Add the cashew nuts and fennel seeds, chilli powder, ginger, coriander and onion. Rub first the ghee and then the beaten egg evenly into the mix. Don't be surprised if the mixture is still very crumbly. Add 3 to 4 tablespoons water gradually, playing it by ear, until you obtain a stiff dough. Shape the dough into walnut-sized balls ready to fry.

Heat the oil in a heavy-bottomed pan until it is very, very hot and carefully drop in your balls in batches. Cook for 3 to 5 minutes until golden.

Drain and serve warm with lime wedges and a tipple of your choice.

RAITA

Cool as you like.

The universal coolant to go with your bhajis and curry, this version is cooler than a polar bear's armpit.

2 large tomatoes
½ cucumber
a thumb-sized piece of ginger, finely chopped
a handful of chopped coriander

1 teaspoon black mustard seeds
3 spring onions, thinly sliced
300ml natural yoghurt

Remove the eye from the tomatoes, place in a bowl and pour over boiling water. Leave to stand for 10 to 15 seconds before draining. Peel away the skin, take out the seeds and finely chop.

Peel the cucumber, scrape out the seeds and finely chop.

Now, simply mix all the ingredients together with some salt and pepper. Serve chilled.

Spoon this mixture on top of the hot dhal. This process is called tempering and it's the Indian equivalent of putting a knob of butter on your mashed potatoes. You can vary this by adding fresh coriander or chillies (if you want it hot) to the mixture.

COCONUT CHUTNEY

This is served at every meal on every table in southern India. It is lovely with curries and nibbles or with some plain rice and a sambar for a delicious, simple meal.

1 tablespoon vegetable oil
1 teaspoon black mustard seeds
8 curry leaves
1 teaspoon urad dhal
½ fresh coconut, grated

a thumb-sized piece of ginger, finely chopped or grated
2 green chillies, finely chopped
½ teaspoon salt

To grate the coconut, either put it through the fine blade on your food processor or through the medium blade of a hand grater.

Heat a small frying pan. Add the oil, mustard seeds, curry leaves and dhal and cook until the dhal turns golden brown. Crush the mixure in a pestle and mortar to break down the dhal.

Tip into a mixing bowl and mix together with everything else. **Voilà**, it's as easy as that.

DHAL   SERVES 4

Dhal is not just a load of old lentils. When cooked properly, it is a great dish. In India, dhal seems to keep body and soul together and although it is often a meal of necessity, thousands of years of culinary magic have made it delicious.

There are various types of dhal and this recipe uses the basic masoor dhal, which is a cross between a lentil and a split pea.

for the top

2 tablespoons ghee
  (or vegetable oil)
½ teaspoon black mustard seeds
½ teaspoon cumin seed
10–15 curry leaves
1 teaspoon garam masala
1 onion, very finely chopped

250g masoor dhal
250g tomatoes
1 onion, chopped
750ml vegetable stock
200ml coconut milk
1 green chilli, finely chopped
3 cloves of garlic, finely chopped
1 teaspoon turmeric
½ teaspoon ground cumin
½ teaspoon ground coriander

Soak the dhal in cold water for 10 minutes, then drain.

Remove the eye from the tomatoes, place in a bowl and pour over boiling water. Leave to stand for 10 to 15 seconds before draining. Peel away the skin and chop.

Add the dhal, tomato, onion, stock, coconut milk, chilli, garlic, turmeric, cumin and coriander to a large heavy-based pan. Bring this mixture to the boil, then reduce the heat and simmer for about 25 to 30 minutes until the dhal is cooked – it should be soft and mushy.

In a frying pan, heat the ghee and put in the mustard and cumin seeds. When they start to pop, add the curry leaves, garam masala and the onion and cook until the onion has softened.

Serve the dhal in an authentic-looking dish with the yummy onions and curry leaves on the top.

ALOO GOBI   SERVES 4

A particular favourite, this vegetable side dish is great to have with bread, rice or for stuffing Indian breads.

2 tablespoons ghee or vegetable oil

1 onion, finely chopped

a thumb-sized piece of ginger, finely chopped or grated

1 teaspoon black mustard seeds

5 curry leaves

½ teaspoon turmeric

½ teaspoon fenugreek seeds

2 green chillies

½ teaspoon chilli powder

3 potatoes, diced into 1cm cubes

½ small cauliflower, split into florets

250g (about 4) tomatoes, chopped

½ teaspoon sugar

½ teaspoon salt

1 teaspoon lemon juice

In a saucepan, warm the ghee or oil and fry the onion until transparent.

Add the ginger, mustard seeds, curry leaves, turmeric, fenugreek, chillies and chilli powder. Cook for 2 minutes, stirring continuously until the seeds start popping.

Add the potatoes and stir through until coated by the spices. Add the cauli, tomatoes, sugar, salt and 2 tablespoons water and simmer for 25 minutes to half an hour. Add the lemon juice, check the seasoning and serve.

BHINDI (OKRA) BHAJI   SERVES 4

Some people are a bit funny about okra, or ladies' fingers as they are sometimes called (though if my lady had fingers like this, we would have to part company). This is because they are sometimes overcooked and slimy . . . indeed a little bit snotty, but we love them. Okra is best cooked quickly to retain its flavour and crunch. A good tip is to try it on a barbecue – it's brilliant.

1 onion, finely chopped
2 tablespoons ghee
  (or vegetable oil if you prefer)
½ teaspoon turmeric
1 teaspoon black mustard seeds
1 teaspoon ground coriander

1 teaspoon ground cumin
10 curry leaves
250g tomatoes
½ teaspoon sugar
500g okra, tops cut off
a squeeze of lemon juice

Fry the onion in the ghee over a medium heat until it slightly changes colour. Add the turmeric, mustard seeds, coriander, cumin and curry leaves and fry for a further 2 minutes, stirring continuously.

Add the tomatoes and the sugar and simmer for 5 minutes. Keeping a medium heat, add the okra and cook, uncovered, for 5 to 7 minutes until tender. Season and add the lemon juice. Serve as a side dish or as part of a vegetarian meal.

YELLOW RICE AND PEAS SERVES 4

Indians love peas and this is my favourite curry rice dish too. It's colourful and tasty – a bit like ourselves. Frozen peas are fine to use and often they're better than fresh because, as the advert says, they are frozen at the moment the pod went 'pop'.

1 tablespoon ghee or vegetable oil
1 onion, finely chopped
1 teaspoon mustard seeds
1 teaspoon cumin seeds
1 teaspoon turmeric
1 cinnamon stick

10 curry leaves
1 red chilli
200g basmati rice
500ml vegetable or chicken stock
100g peas

In a saucepan with a lid, heat the ghee or oil and cook the onion until it is transparent. Add the mustard seeds, cumin seeds, turmeric, cinnamon stick, curry leaves and the whole chilli. Stir for 1 minute until the spices are well coated with the oil.

Stir in the rice and cook for 1 minute. Add the stock, cover and simmer for 20 minutes. Finally add the peas and let them heat through. Fluff up and serve.

SOUTH INDIAN PRAWN CURRY SERVES 4

This is a spicy, dry curry that balances the sweetness of the tamarind with the heat of the chillies, the thick sauce clinging to the prawns. We've used desiccated coconut in this one, but they usually use fresh coconut in Kerala, which is also delicious.

2 tablespoons vegetable oil
1 onion, finely chopped
a thumb-sized piece of ginger,
  finely chopped
3 cloves of garlic, chopped
2 green chillies, seeded and
  finely chopped
4 tomatoes, chopped

1 teaspoon turmeric
1 teaspoon tamarind paste
1 teaspoon honey
2 tablespoons desiccated coconut
500g peeled raw prawns
a small bunch of fresh coriander,
  chopped

Heat the oil in a frying pan and cook the onion until translucent.

Add the ginger, garlic and chilli, stir and cook for 1 minute. Add the tomato, turmeric, tamarind paste and honey and mix thoroughly. Leave to cook slowly for 10 minutes until the sauce is a little less liquid. Add the coconut and stir.

Add the prawns and cook for 4 to 5 minutes (do not overcook or they will become rubbery). Taste and season.

Sprinkle with the coriander. This curry is great with some simple rice and chapatis.

VEGETABLE CURRY SERVES 4

This is a great recipe and a curry that non-veggies will enjoy too. So often the vegetable curry is an apology to keep the vegetarians happy, but this isn't, the delicious blend of spices and coconut milk making it a very tasty concoction. Ooh, I could hug a tree.

4 tablespoons ghee
  (or vegetable oil)

2 large onions

3 teaspoons garam masala

1 teaspoon turmeric

1 teaspoon cumin seeds

15 curry leaves

200g aubergines, chopped into
  thick cubes

500g sweet potatoes chopped into
  thick cubes

4 cloves of garlic, finely chopped

a thumb-sized piece of ginger,
  finely chopped

3 green chillies
  (adjust the amount to your taste)

2 large carrots, chopped

290ml vegetable stock

400g tin of tomatoes

100ml coconut milk

2 teaspoons sugar

½ small cauliflower,
  split into florets

200g whole button mushrooms

100g peas

a large handful of chopped coriander

In a large pan, heat the ghee, add the onion and cook over a low heat until translucent. Add the garam masala, turmeric, cumin and curry leaves and cook for 2 minutes.

Add the aubergine, sweet potato, garlic, ginger and the whole chillies (so you can fish them out at the end or eat them if you're feeling daft). Cook for 5 minutes, stirring continuously to coat the veg in the spices.

Add the carrot, stock, tomatoes, coconut milk and sugar. Cover and cook on a low heat for a further 20 minutes, stirring frequently, or until the carrot is tender and the other ingredients have married together.

When the sweet potato is nearly cooked, add the cauliflower and mushrooms. Cook for a further 7 to 10 minutes, then add the peas and cook for a final 2 minutes.

Season and garnish with the coriander just before you serve.

CRUNCHY PALAK PANEER   SERVES 4

Paneer is a fresh cheese used extensively in vegetarian Indian cooking. You should be able to find it in a big supermarket or Asian grocery store. It carries flavours very well and the texture is fantastic. Palak is an Indian word for spinach.

for the sauce

2 tablespoons ghee
  (or vegetable oil)
2 onions, finely chopped
a thumb-sized piece of ginger,
  finely chopped
3 cloves of garlic, chopped
1 teaspoon ground cumin
1 teaspoon ground coriander
1 teaspoon turmeric
1 whole green chilli
1 teaspoon salt
400g tin of chopped tomatoes
1 teaspoon sugar
500g fresh spinach, washed

to coat the paneer

2 teaspoons garam masala
50g semolina
200g paneer, cut into
  Oxo-sized cubes

vegetable oil, for shallow frying
a small handful of chopped fresh
  coriander leaves
1 teaspoon lemon juice

In a saucepan, heat the ghee, then add the onion and cook for about 3 minutes until soft.

Add the ginger and garlic and cook for a further minute. Add the cumin, coriander, turmeric, the whole chilli and the salt and cook and stir for a minute to infuse all the spices.

Add the chopped tomatoes and sugar and simmer for 10 minutes.

Meanwhile, in a mixing bowl combine the garam masala and semolina. Into the bowl place the cubes of paneer and coat (it's the old crisp roast potato vibe).

Heat enough oil to cover the bottom of a frying pan and fry the paneer until crisp and golden.

Now, back to the saucepan. Add the spinach and 2 tablespoons water to the tomato sauce and stir in, cooking until wilted.

Fold in your crunchy paneer and sprinkle over the coriander and lemon juice. Serve with a smile and a happy face!

DUCK MADRAS CURRY   SERVES 4

When we were in Chennai (which up to a couple of years ago was called Madras) we went out looking for a classic chicken Madras and guess what, it didn't seem to exist. So we got to thinking that as we like a Madras made with potatoes, if you did it with duck you would have all that lovely duck fat going into your spicy potatoes. It's a rich dish but fantastic, so duck off down to the butcher's and make this for a special dinner.

1 duck, portioned (ask your butcher to do this or buy portions)

3 onions, sliced

2 teaspoons coriander seeds

2 teaspoons cumin seeds

1 teaspoon fennel seeds

6 cardamom pods, bruised (i.e. gently bashed with a rolling pin or in a pestle and mortar)

1 cinnamon stick

10 cloves of garlic, cut chunky

a thumb-sized piece of ginger, finely chopped

4 potatoes, cut chunky

10 curry leaves

5 dried whole chillies

1½ teaspoons turmeric

400ml coconut milk

200ml chicken stock

1 teaspoon tamarind paste

In a dry frying pan (there will be enough fat coming out of the duck) brown the duck, then lift out and set aside. In the duck fat left in the pan, cook the onion until golden.

Whilst this is happening, in a dry frying pan dry roast the coriander, cumin, fennel, cardamom and cinnamon to release their flavour.

To the onion, add the garlic, ginger, potato, curry leaves, chillies, turmeric and the dry-roasted whole spices. Cook for a couple of minutes, stirring so everything is roughly coated.

Add the coconut milk, stock and tamarind. Cover and simmer gently for 45 minutes, then turn up the heat a notch and cook with the lid off for another 15 minutes.

CARDAMOM CHICKEN

SERVES 4–6 (DEPENDING ON THE SIZE OF YOUR BIRD)

One of our all-time favourites. Driving through the Cardamom Hills, we pulled over at a wholesaler selling cardamoms. The women were using woven baskets to sift through the pods, grading the little green lovelies, while the men brought in huge sacks of them to keep everyone busy. The overwhelming memory is the smell and colour of one of the most beautiful areas of southern India.

3 tablespoons ghee
  (or vegetable oil)
1 chicken, portioned (ask your
  butcher to do this or buy portions)
2 onions, chopped
25 cardamom pods
4 whole red chillies
a thumb-sized piece of ginger,
  finely chopped

4 cloves of garlic, chopped
200ml full-fat natural yoghurt
400ml coconut milk
1 teaspoon salt
3 tablespoons lemon juice
a handful of chopped
  fresh coriander

Heat the ghee in a saucepan and brown the chicken portions for 5 to 6 minutes (do not burn!). Remove the chicken from the pan and set aside. In the same pan, cook the onion until golden.

Meanwhile, bash the cardamom pods and extract the seeds (gently does it), then bruise the seeds in a pestle and mortar, having discarded the husks.

Add the cardamom seeds, chillies, ginger and garlic to the pan and cook for 1 minute. Return the chicken portions to the pan and coat well with the spice mixture.

Add the yoghurt, coconut milk, salt and lemon zest. Bring to the boil, cover and simmer for 20 minutes. Remove the lid and cook for a further 10 minutes until the sauce has thickened.

Add the coriander and lemon juice, stir through and heat for a minute. Season to taste and serve.

SOUTHERN INDIAN DRY MASALA
FISH CURRY WITH A CHUTNEY   SERVES 4

This dish is great served with our yellow rice and peas or fab on the barbecue with a nice salad.

for the fish bit

4 nice thick white fish fillets
(monkfish, haddock, hake, cod
or something similar)

3 tablespoons (about 1 small pot)
natural yoghurt

2 teaspoons garam masala

1 teaspoon black mustard seeds

1 teaspoon ground coriander

1 teaspoon ground cumin

½ teaspoon chilli powder

6 cardamom pods, bruised
(i.e. gently bashed with a rolling
pin or in a pestle and mortar)

½ teaspoon salt

1 tablespoon vegetable oil

for the chutney

1 tablespoon vegetable oil

1 onion, finely chopped

a thumb-sized piece of ginger,
cut chunky

6 cloves of garlic, finely chopped

1 green chilli, chopped

10 curry leaves

1½ tablespoons desiccated coconut

400g tin of tomatoes

2 teaspoons sugar

2 teaspoons balsamic vinegar

Wash the fish and blot dry.

In a mixing bowl, mix together the yoghurt, garam masala, mustard seeds, coriander, cumin, chilli, cardamom and the salt. Add the fish, coat with the marinade and leave for about an hour.

While the fish is marinating, make the chutney. In a saucepan, heat the oil, add the onion and cook until soft. Add the ginger, garlic, chilli, curry leaves and coconut. Cook for a couple of minutes until the coconut has browned.

Add the tomatoes, sugar and balsamic vinegar and simmer, uncovered, for about 20 to 30 minutes until the chutney has reduced to a thick, sticky goo.

In a frying pan, heat the tablespoon of vegetable oil. When hot, shake off the excess marinade from the fish and fry for 3 to 5 minutes each side until golden.

Top the fish with the warm chutney and eat with gusto (sorry, we have no recipe for gusto!).

VEGETABLE BIRYANI

SERVES 4 HUNGRY BIKERS OR 6 NORMAL PEOPLE

An all-in-one vegetarian dish, it's the way the vegetable curry steams through the rice that prevents any flavours being wasted. The saffron-infused milk adds a psychedelic colour scheme as well as a special taste.

3 tablespoons ghee
  (or vegetable oil)
2 onions, finely chopped
2 teaspoons garam masala
1 teaspoon black mustard seeds
3 whole green chillies
4 cloves of garlic, finely chopped
1 teaspoon ground coriander
1 teaspoon ground cumin
a thumb-sized piece of ginger,
  finely chopped
1 teaspoon salt
3 potatoes, chopped
2 large carrots, chopped
¼ cauliflower, cut into florets
3 large tomatoes, chopped
200g button mushrooms
100g French beans, chopped
a good handful of chopped fresh
  coriander leaves

for the top
2 tablespoons thick natural yoghurt
3 tablespoons milk
a pinch of saffron
50g butter

for the rice bit
500ml vegetable stock
400g basmati rice
10 cardamom pods, bruised
  (i.e. gently bashed with a rolling
  pin or in a pestle and mortar)
20 curry leaves
1 cinnamon stick, halved
150g frozen peas

In a saucepan, heat the ghee and fry the onion until golden. Add the garam masala, mustard seeds, chillies, garlic, coriander, cumin, ginger and salt. Stir and cook for a minute until the seeds start to pop.

Stir in the potato, carrot, cauliflower, tomato, mushrooms and French beans, add 8 tablespoons water and bring to the boil. Cover and simmer gently for 45 minutes.

Meanwhile, to make the top, mix the yoghurt, milk and saffron together in a bowl. Leave to infuse.

Preheat the oven to 170°C.

To make the rice bit, place the stock in a saucepan and bring to the boil. Add the rice, cardamom, curry leaves and cinnamon stick. The rice only needs to be partly cooked, so simmer for just 5 minutes or until the stock is absorbed. Stir in the peas.

To assemble your biryani, pour half the vegetable curry into an ovenproof or casserole dish. On top of this, place half the rice. Next, pour in the remaining curry and top with the remaining rice.

Finally, pour on the saffron and yoghurt mixture in a random pattern and dot the top with knobs of butter. This way, you will get layers of rice and curry all topped with the golden marbling from the saffron. Cover with foil and then a tight lid.

Place the biryani in the oven for 45 minutes or until the rice is cooked. Serve with chapatis, raita and chutney.

STRAWBERRY SHRIKHAND SERVES 4

Shrikhand is a rich Indian yoghurt pudding, which we've served over strawberries soaked in caster sugar and balsamic vinegar. It's a very exotic strawberries and cream, so you don't need much.

for the shrikhand
a pinch of saffron
4 cardamom pods
250ml Greek-style natural yoghurt
3 tablespoons caster sugar
25g flaked almonds, toasted

for the strawberries
250g strawberries
2 teaspoons caster sugar
2 teaspoons balsamic vinegar

Firstly, soak the saffron in 1 tablespoon boiling water. Bash the cardamom pods in a pestle and mortar to release the seeds and crush them. Discard the husks.

Take the tops off the strawberries and cut in two. Place in a bowl with the caster sugar and balsamic vinegar. Cover with clingfilm and leave to steep for an hour.

In a bowl, mix together the yoghurt, ground cardamom seeds, saffron (and saffron water) and the caster sugar.

Spoon the strawberries into four sundae glasses. Top with the shrikhand and sprinkle over the toasted almonds. (To toast the almonds, put them in a dry frying pan over a medium heat, keeping your beady eye on them as they will burn very easily. Shake the pan from time to time to keep them moving. Or buy them ready-toasted.)

This is great served with shortbread biscuits.

BANANA, CARDAMOM AND VANILLA LASSI **MAKES 2 GLASSES**

A lassi is a delicious yoghurt-based drink, which is great on a hot day or for quaffing with an Indian meal. Lassis traditionally come in two ways – salt or sweet. The sweet is a lovely drink, while the salt goes well with food (and is great for a jippy tum). More modern restaurants also now make fruit lassis, like mango and pineapple and our banana and cardamom. This smoothest of smoothies is a fantastic energy drink and would even serve as a quick breakfast.

2 cardamom pods
2 ripe bananas
2 teaspoons honey
200ml natural yoghurt
200ml milk
3 drops of vanilla extract
ice

Bash the cardamom pods in a pestle and mortar to release the seeds and place the seeds in a blender.

Place all the other ingredients apart from the ice in the blender and blitz. Serve in two tall glasses over ice.

MASALA ICED COFFEE   MAKES 4 GLASSES

In India, you get something called a masala coffee, which is
a coffee with spices like cardamoms and cloves. We made our
own masala coffee and discovered it can be turned into brilliant
iced coffee.

750ml milk

2 tablespoons sugar

1 vanilla pod, split

a thumb-sized piece of ginger,
  finely chopped

2 tablespoons good,
  fresh ground coffee (not Nescaff!)

5 cardamom pods, bruised
  (i.e. gently bashed with a rolling
  pin or in a pestle and mortar)

1 cinnamon stick

ice

cocoa powder, for dusting

Put the milk and sugar into a saucepan with the vanilla pod, bring to the
boil and keep warm over a low heat.

In a dry frying pan, dry roast the ginger for 1 minute, and then grind in
a pestle and mortar. Add to the milk with the coffee, bruised cardamom
pods and cinnamon. Cover and leave to infuse for at least 5 minutes.
Strain off all the solids and leave the coffee to cool. When cool, chill in the
refrigerator.

Pour the coffee with a flourish from one jug to another to get a froth going
and then serve in long glasses over ice. Dust the top of each glass with a
sprinkle of cocoa powder.

GOLDEN CARDAMOM MARTINI   MAKES 1

Anytime, anyplace, anywhere, get one of these down your neck. It makes a lovely aperitif before your Indian big night in.

35ml gin
35ml dry vermouth
ice
10 cardamom pods
a pinch of saffron

First, think like James Bond – sophisticated and suave.

Pour the gin and vermouth over ice in a cocktail shaker (or a container with a screw-topped lid). Crack the cardamoms in a pestle and mortar to release the tiny seeds and add to the shaker with the saffron, then shake until your teeth start to feel loose.

Strain and serve with some poppadoms to nibble.

ARGENTINA

C H I L E

N

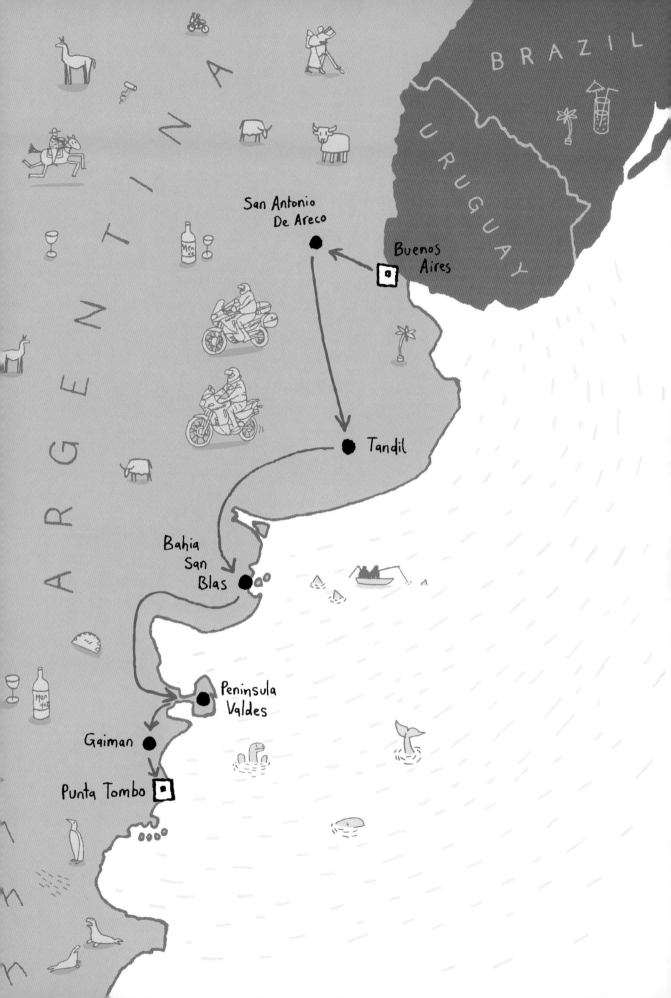

DAVE:

People who sell things at traffic lights can tell you a lot about a local culture. Evening papers are for the work obsessed and information hungry; tired carnations are aimed at late-working, guilty husbands; lucky heather at the superstitious. It's the quintessential impulse buy: in thirty seconds you can only sell something that the buyer really thinks they need.

At the traffic lights in Buenos Aires, they were selling footballs.

Think about it. You've had a tough day in the office or been on your feet in the shop since breakfast, and a kid approaches you with a bag full of Nike knock-offs.

'Yeah, two please.'

Not for the first time in this amazing country, a grin spread over our faces. The spirit of Argentina? Here it was.

w, the thing that really strikes you about Argentina ts size. It's the eighth largest country in the world. etching out from the tropical north right down uth to the icy glaciers of the Antarctic. It even has me mountains to the west (the Andes) and its own sert (the Patagonian). It's just a whopper.

With so much to choose from, we had to narrow our trip down. The obvious place to start was where our plane landed, Buenos Aires. From there, we wanted to stride out into the grassy pampas in search of that iconic South American cowboy, the gaucho. After a last tango back in the capital, we were to head south (well, it's me age) to Patagonia. A massive area that covers pretty much all of the tip of South America, we were searching for the most amazing wildlife on the planet and the

'Buenos Aires is a stunning city and the whole thing feels very European, 'Like Barcelona on steroids,' as Dave put it.' SI

LANDING IN BUENOS AIRES

SI: Buenos Aires is a stunning city and the whole thing feels very European, 'Like Barcelona on steroids,' as Dave put it. When we arrived in late October, spring was in the air and the stylish boulevards were laden with jacaranda blossoms, the purple flowers lining street after street. What strikes you everywhere are the wealth and confidence that lie behind its buildings, constant reminders that Argentina was once the seventh-richest nation in the world.

DAVE: What a city, what a circus, oh what a show . . . sorry, I was off on one a bit then. This is the best city I have ever been to. It really works. The streets and boulevards are tree-lined and wide and the Avenida 9 de Julio is in fact the widest street in the world, with eighteen lanes of traffic. When the lights change it really is a case of, 'Run Forrest, run.' The last time I saw Si move so fast was when his giro blew away.

SI: We got hold of our bikes in Buenos Aires from a great company called Motocare whose proprietor, Mariano, was fantastic. We hired two Honda 650 Transalps with full luggage and Mariano threw in a few spares and a puncture repair kit.

Around the cities, the highways are wide and fast, but the driving, careless with no quarter given to bikes of any description, not even those carrying takeaway food (and GOD, do the Argentinians love their food). We proceeded with care initially and then got stuck into the vibe of riding in Buenos Aires. You know what it's like. You're sat in a taxi thinking, 'S**t this looks a bit full on,' but when you're on the bike and in the traffic, you just deal with it and end up having a really good time.

But the biggest danger in Buenos Aires is not the traffic, it's the girls – THEY'RE LEGENDARY!! Perfectly formed, they have bums like Kylie and wear jeans that are as tight as the skin on a salami (it's all the beef they eat, I'm convinced). Dave and I had more than a little cause to lose concentration while riding, though you must understand that our owl-like necks have been developed over many years and all in the name of research. Our colleague Sam Squire told me to tell the lady readers that the blokes were fit as well. I must confess, I didn't notice.

IN SEARCH OF
THE GAUCHO

DAVE: Tango, steak and football are the things that come to most people's minds when Argentina is mentioned, and although we often find on our travels how misleading national stereotypes can be, there's certainly something there that does define the Argentine character. But standing tall behind this holy trinity is the country's shadowy national figure: the gaucho.

The gaucho was the original cowboy, long before John Wayne and Roy Rogers got in on the act. A solitary figure, with vast herds of cattle and sheep to control, wild horses to capture and tame and even vaster prairies to graze them all on, his life was his horse, his bedroll and his facón, a wickedly long knife tucked into the back of his belt.

Expert in the saddle, his horse was as much a part of the man as his legs were. He would hunt on horseback, armed with a lasso or boleadoras, a thong with three heavy balls that he used to capture horses and cattle. So it was that, with his balls spinning around his head, the gaucho was a happy man.

Like the men of Barrow-in-Furness, the gaucho was also a stylish dresser in those baggy pleated trousers that button at the ankles (I had a pair like that in the days of the New Romantics . . . not for long, though). Add a neckerchief, two belts, a set of spurs, beret and a vest, then top it all off with a poncho and that's some outfit to go to the bingo in. But let's be fair, it was a tough life out on those pampas.

The gauchos' lives changed profoundly, though, when the pampas became privately owned. Estancias and ranches were built; meaning gauchos were now labelled trespassers and cattle thieves. With this new order, they found employment as hired ranch hands, but never lost their pride, dignity and traditions (they refused to do any labour that involved them dismounting from their horses, something they saw as being beneath them).

ARGENTINA

Today, the gaucho has come to embody a kind of ruthless romanticism that you still sense in the tango halls, on the terraces worshipping Boca Juniors, or even among the parrillas (barbecues) along the riverfront at Puerto Madero. The Argentinians are a proud people who have known more than their share of sadness and disaster, but who still sit tall in the saddle, riding out with renewed self-belief into each new day.

So, it was in search of the true gaucho spirit that we found ourselves riding into San Antonio de Areco, a couple of hours from Buenos Aires. It's a small pampas town that every year hosts an impressive gaucho festival with parades, displays of horsemanship and lots of open-air cooking. Sadly, it was more like surfing than riding the day we rode into town. The rain was coming down in bucket loads and as we approached the centre, we passed a long column of horseboxes and pickups heading in the opposite direction. The festival had finally been abandoned because of the rainstorm and our only sight of a gaucho was one old bloke standing forlornly under an awning, wondering where he'd left his horse.

> 'The gaucho was the original cowboy, long before John Wayne and Roy Rogers got in on the act. A solitary figure, with vast herds of cattle and sheep to control, wild horses to capture and tame and even vaster prairies to graze them all on.'
> DAVE

We're bikers, so we're used to getting wet. But there's wet and there's absolutely hosed, when you get off your bike and the only dry bit of your body is the inside of your mouth. Which is how Argentina's first real sight of Kingy was him changing his underpants in the town square. Fortunately the local constabulary were holed up somewhere warm out of the rain, otherwise our Argentina trip might have been over very quickly indeed.

'One by one, the crew announced that they'd never eaten a steak like it, and this was in a little local restaurant, not a swanky Buenos Aires establishment.' SI

THE BEEF

SI: Film crews are used to working in all weathers, but with no gauchos to film, we reluctantly retired to a nearby pulperia and forced ourselves to eat and drink for several hours till the storm passed. A pulperia is a combination of a general store and pub, where traditionally a gaucho would ride in for a session of wine, women and song. This one had been beautifully restored and turned into a cracking restaurant, and the silence that fell as the crew feasted on their first proper Argentine steaks was impressive.

Let's be clear about this, Argentina is carnivore heaven. People eat unbelievable quantities of meat, at all times of the day, and with no great need for accompanying vegetables or sauces. But none of this is surprising once you get to taste it – the quality of the meat is incredible. One by one, the crew announced that they'd never eaten a steak like it, and this was in a little local restaurant, not a swanky Buenos Aires establishment. And the wine wasn't half bad either.

It was a useful introduction to the joys of Argentine meat because the next day we found ourselves on a nearby ranch learning how to cook an asado. An asado is a megabarbie where huge cuts of meat (in this case a whole lamb and a side of beef) are cooked slowly over a fire, along with sausages, kidneys, delicious morcillas (black puddings) and any other bits they can lay their hands on. Under the watchful eye of Samuel, the asado masterchef, we managed to put together a meaty feast for the gauchos of the estate, who'd been out in the saddle all day.

Now, you have never seen the bones of two animals picked clean in such a short space of time. It was like one of those David Attenborough films where a squirrel falls into a river full of piranhas. At the end of the meal, the moon rose, the guitars appeared and Dave looked like the cat that had not just got the cream, but polished off the whole dairy.

ARGENTINA

'it's an attitude, a style, steamy hot and ultracool.'
DAVE

THE TANGO

DAVE: Back in Buenos Aires, we continued to do our best for the Argentine beef industry. In our favourite restaurant, La Brigada, the waiter even cut our steaks with a spoon, just to demonstrate how tender they were. And in a moment of madness, quite possibly brought on by the protein overload racing round our bodies, we decided it was time to tango.

Tango is a world I was born into, except in the maternity hospital they mistakenly fitted me with two left feet, no co-ordination and an inability to concentrate without sticking my tongue out. This makes my future life as a tango gigolo a bit doubtful.

Tango has its origins at the end of the nineteenth century, when boatloads of European immigrants began to arrive. At first, it was the music of the night. The brothel was a popular spot for the working classes and while customers sat in the waiting rooms marking time before they went up to the diving board, musicians would play songs with racy lyrics and the men would dance with the working girls. So it was that the tango developed: a promise of what was to come.

In the twentieth century, the tango spilled out on to the streets. Dancing the tango allowed you to be more intimate with strangers than society generally allowed, hence its popularity. Tango halls opened and the dance became popular with everyone except the disapproving upper classes. The brothels turned into cabaret halls and stars were made of the tango dancers.

The tango is not just a series of dance steps; it's an attitude, a style, steamy hot and ultracool at the same time. We wanted to try and do it properly, not take the mick, so we signed up with Inés. Inés taught tango in a lovely tree-lined square in the old San Telmo district. She was a great teacher, spoke good English and, unfortunately, was stunningly attractive. I say 'unfortunately' because the tango is a difficult enough dance to get right at the best of times, and it's even harder when your partner looks like Inés.

'Keep watching my feet,' she commanded as she steered Kingy round the square.

'I was trying to,' he admitted later, 'but she had a low-cut dress in the way.'

I reckon she deserves a medal for bravery too. How her feet didn't get crushed by an eighteen-stone Geordie in motorcycle boots, I'll never know.

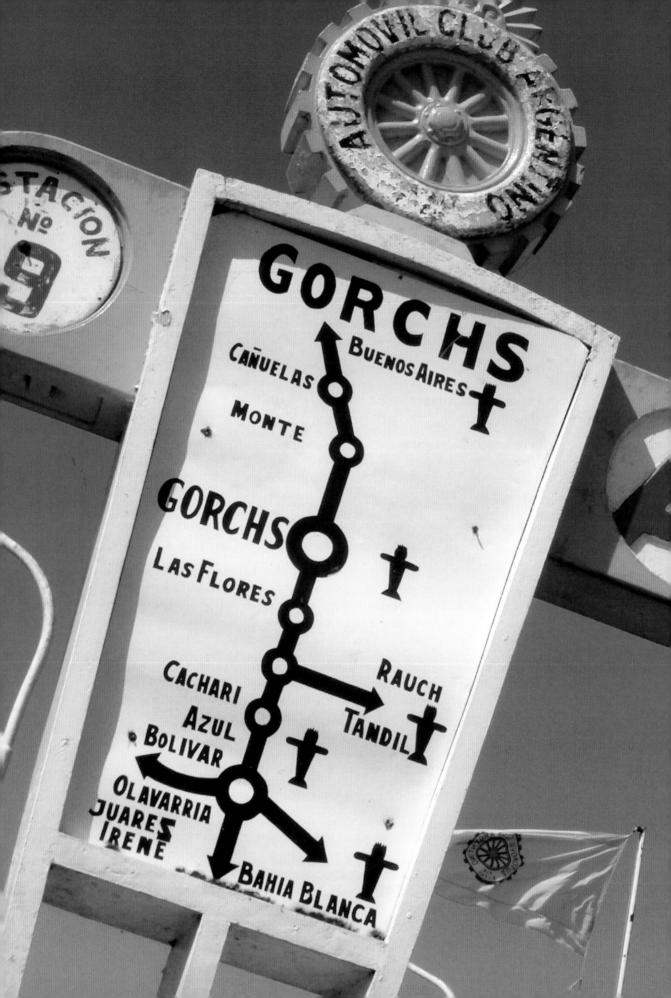

HEADING SOUTH

SI: As so often happens after a few days in a big city, even one as enjoyable as Buenos Aires, we started to miss the open road. It was time to stuff the tango CDs in the panniers and open the throttle, to head south through the endless grasslands of the pampas. We knew we could only scratch the surface of this vast country, but even to do that was going to involve some serious biking. Time to get going.

There are a few things you need to get your head around if you're ever going to ride in Argentina. Firstly, the country is HUGE, so pick your route carefully, get a good map and always, always carry spare fuel and water. When Dave and I rode through the pampas on our way south we encountered strong headwinds, which knocked the fuel economy of the bikes through the floor (and dried you out like the skin on a pensioner's bunion).

Secondly, the further south you go, the colder it gets, so pack your windstopper and your woolly knickers – even if they do itch. Finally, it's difficult to keep your concentration on the long straight roads, so work out a way of amusing yourself. Keep in mind that Argentina has the worst traffic accident record in the whole of South America (if statistics are to be believed), so you're concentrating not just for you, but for all those space cadets that use the roads.

Riding out of Buenos Aires across the vast open spaces of the pampas was an amazing feeling. With the occasional estancia glimpsed in the distance up an avenue of poplars, we felt like modern-day gauchos riding across the range to find – well, LUNCH!

TATTOO YOU, CHE GUEVARA

SI: Heading south, the countryside changed dramatically. Gone were the rolling grasslands of the pampas and in their place was the scrub and sand of Patagonia.

We were heading for the Peninsula Valdés, situated at the top end of Patagonia and a place for wildlife and birds – and that's just the bars! No, it really is the place to watch whales and elephant seals (no, no, real elephant seals, not me and Dave sunbathing). As the hundred-kilometre digits kept rolling past on the speedo, we caught glimpses of wildlife rushing by: llama-like guanacos, sheep trundling through the thorn bushes, rabbits, hares, even an ostrich with her chicks only metres from the carriageway.

But something was preying on my mind: I had just turned forty and was having a bit of a mid-life crisis. For a long time I had promised myself that if I ever had the good fortune to visit Argentina, I wanted a real keepsake:

'But something was preying on my mind: I had just turned forty and was having a bit of a mid-life crisis . . .' SI

a tattoo. But not just any tattoo. I wanted one of Che Guevara, a son of Argentina and a major influence on my life since, at the age of fourteen, I first read the quote, 'The true revolutionary is guided by great feelings of love.'

So, as Dave and I rode into Puerto Madryn, the nearest big town to the peninsula, there it was, a tattoo parlour blasting out Led Zeppelin. It had to be. Dave looked confused:

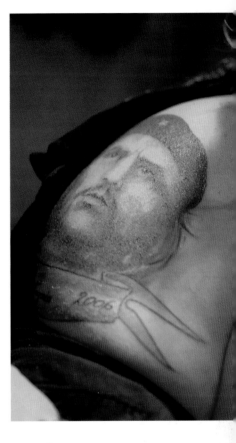

'What ye doing, Kingy?'

'Getting a tattoo.'

'What, now?'

'If I can.'

'You've got to make an appointment. Ye can't just walk in off the street.'

'You did when you got that terrible fish tattooed on your arm.'

'Yeah, but that was in Darlington. We're in Pata-bloody-gonia, ye looney. What do you want done?'

'Che Guevara.'

'Oh, you're serious then.'

'Yes, definitely. Do you fancy it?'

'Narrr.'

'Go on.'

'Yeah, all right.'

That's the good thing about my mate Dave, when he says no, he never, ever means it.

We were pushed for time and, as Dave said, the tattooist sent us away until he was ready with a pencil to devise a design. Dave got the design spot on. Neither of us wanted a pop icon Che, that's not what he was about. We wanted the intensity of a man committed to political change.

We sat for three hours while a man with needles and ink inflicted pain. Never let it be said that a tattoo doesn't hurt. It does! The pain kind of builds. They start with the outlining first, which is the worst bit, then they start filling and shading. Not so bad, but after three hours of it you start to sweat a bit, then you drift off to the sounds of Pearl Jam, the lads bring in beer and all the pain is forgotten.

WALES

DAVE: Patagonia is one of those daft places that you're never quite sure exists. It sounds so far away and eccentric. It is indeed both of these things, and it's a place we have always wanted to visit.

Patagonia is massive, remote and didn't have any riches to speak of, which meant that the Mapuche and Tehuelche tribes that lived there were largely ignored by the conquistadores who, like magpies, loved a bit of bling and were searching the rest of the country for silver. It was our old friend the Portuguese explorer Ferdinand Magellan who gave Patagonia its name. In 1520 he met a Mapuche Indian and exclaimed, 'Cor blimey, look at the size of his feet!' (rough translation). So his sailors nicknamed the land 'Patagones', meaning 'big foot'. Well, this may just be legend, but I like the sound of it.

Colonization of Patagonia from this point on has been a bit spasmodic, but the most important arrivals were, strangely, the Welsh. With the spirit of Charlotte Church on a big night out, the boyos came over in the latter half of the nineteenth century. We visited the towns of Gaiman and Trelew and the Welsh influence is everywhere. When you drive down the street you see signs like 'Dafyd Thomas, mechanic' or 'Jones the Barber'. There are Welsh tearooms, Welsh choirs and an annual Eisteddfod, where Welsh folk from the old country meet up with the chief druid and have a beano. Like Wales, Patagonia also has brilliant lamb.

ARGENTINA

AND WHALES

DAVE: Si and I had never seen a whale and believe me, nothing you've seen in books or on the telly can really prepare you for the experience. Peninsula Valdés is an astonishing place; a UNESCO World Heritage Site that is teeming with wildlife, from southern right whales to penguins and awesome eighteen-foot-long elephant seals.

The undisputed kings, or rather queens, of the Peninsula Valdés are, however, those whales. I'd always imagined whale watching to involve some powerful binoculars and a glimpse of a waterspout about a mile away. So when the first giant shape rose lazily to the surface alongside our boat, Si and I were, for once, completely speechless. And then its mother, five times the size, appeared alongside it.

We were fortunate to be in the company of Tito Bottazzi, whose family have been studying and visiting the whale colonies all their lives. His daughter Robina reeled off a list of facts that grew ever more astonishing. They can weigh up to 60 tonnes, grow to 16 metres long and the calves need 500 litres of their mother's milk a day. But impressive though the details were, the reality of these massive creatures was what took the breath away. They seemed almost pleased to see Tito, gracefully sliding under the boat to appear on the other side, while some particularly overexcited calves burst up through the surface into the air in a display of mad, salty gymnastics.

'Bloody hell,' said Kingy. He opened his mouth to add something, then closed it again. 'Bloody hell,' he said again, after a while. There really wasn't much else you could say. We just felt like the luckiest blokes alive.

THE FOOD

DAVE: Sometimes when we go to a country like Argentina that doesn't have an obvious food culture, we can have a bit of a panic. Well, a big part of our show is food. We all know about Argentinian beef, but what if that was it? The interesting twist is that very often countries whose food has evolved by combining what nature gave them with the melting pot of different settlers' food cultures end up producing really interesting, unique food. This was the case with Argentina.

THE BARBECUE

The starting point does have to be the beef. I think it's the best beef in the world, and this coming from a man who lived in Aberdeenshire for fifteen years with its fantastic Aberdeen Angus steaks. There was a time in Argentina when steak, a by-product of the leather industry, was thrown away; even the poorest person could eat it twice a day. By World War One, though, thousands of tons of bully beef were being exported to Europe to feed the troops, and towns like the infamous Fray Bentos thrived on beef.

The reason why Argentinian beef is so good is that the cattle roam freely and are grass fed. The beef is hung properly and then cooked with skill. Cooking meat in Argentina means only one thing: the parrilla (barbecue). The most common cuts of steak are the lomo, which is our fillet, and the chorizo, which is a rump steak, not a spicy Spanish sausage. People like their beef cooked 'a punto', which is just the rare side of medium, and cooks here have the knack of getting the meat to the perfect point where the middle is still just a little pink. This seems to suit the beef here well, especially the chorizo, which in my opinion does need a little cooking.

> 'Beef is a big deal in Argentina and this cannot be denied.'
> **DAVE**

They also have T-bones, massive beef ribs and strips of skirt steak nearly a metre long, which serve just one person. The portions are massive. In a Patagonian cookbook I found, the portions are truly biker-sized. One recipe for rib-eye suggests an 8lb piece of beef would serve six! They are also very fussy about the fuel they use, which is always hardwood charcoal.

Down by the river in Buenos Aires, a cloud of smoke hangs over the waterfront. At first you think it's a fire, until you catch the aromatic smell of wood smoke and roasting meat. These are rows of parrilla stands all selling lunchtime barbecues. It's an everyday way of life and we were impressed as pretty secretaries poured out from office buildings and bought a hunk of meat that would feed a family. They would sit down and demolish the whole joint without even smudging their lipstick. These were our sort of women . . . and I bet they could dance the tango as well.

The parrilla is often burning alongside a big open fire called an asado. Around this are metal crosses and frames on which a whole lamb or goat is spatchcocked the same way you would a chicken. This is outdoor cooking on a massive scale, and when done skilfully there is nothing better. On the parrilla they will cook kidneys and sausage. Wonderful black pudding is on the menu and sweetbreads are also a favourite here, marinated for an hour in lemon juice and then cooked gently, ending up juicy with a subtle taste (just a note: sweetbreads are not testicles, but two types of thyroid gland). They also cook up the testicles, which taste like a plate of old balls.

Beef is a big deal in Argentina and this cannot be denied, but down south in Patagonia, lamb is the main thing. It is eaten here when it is very young and lean and anything over six months they would term as mutton. It is superb.

'Down by the river in Buenos Aires, a cloud of smoke hangs over the waterfront. At first you think it's a fire, until you catch the aromatic smell of wood smoke and roasting meat.' DAVE

> 'Argentina is the fourth biggest wine producer in the world, behind France, Italy and Spain (in that order), and it's very, very good stuff. The wine industry is newish, but the country has such a diverse climate and good soil that wine production of every type is possible.' DAVE

WINE

Argentina is the fourth biggest wine producer in the world, behind France, Italy and Spain (in that order), and it's very, very good stuff. The wine industry is newish, but the country has such a diverse climate and good soil that wine production of every type is possible. The devaluation of the peso also made wine cheap to export, so now Argentina exports more than it consumes domestically.

In Argentina, red wine is a way of life. It first arrived in Argentina when a priest brought vine stalks from Chile in the mid-sixteenth century. It's a bit of a Jack-and-the-beanstalk story because the frugal offerings he planted in Mendoza flourished and now supply ninety percent of Argentina's wine. With its advantageous terrain, irrigated by pollution-free waters from the slopes of the Andes, it turns out that the province of Mendoza is vineyard heaven. Word soon spread and within the next couple of hundred years the rumour on the block was that the wine from Argentina was better than that at home in Spain.

The star of Argentinian wine is, without a doubt, the red wine produced from the Malbec grape. Argentinian Malbec, with its notes of spice and blackcurrant, is the mark by which all other Malbecs are judged. But I don't want to do Argentinian wine growers a disservice because they do produce a complete range of wines. The Argentinian Merlot is very good, with a hoofing whiff of bananas, and although the majority of wines are red, where whites are concerned they do a good Sauvignon, full of gooseberries, and an excellent Chardonnay, nice, mellow and not oaked.

MATÉ

Anyway, that's enough Oz Clarke. The other great drink in Argentina is maté. Maté, a bit like green tea, is a national institution. It's made from the dried, cured leaves of the Paraguayan holly tree and delivers a powerful caffeine kick. But it's much more than a mid-morning pick-you-up.

The drink started with the gauchos. They would drink maté to stave off hunger pains and to give them energy out on the pampas. The ritual is very important. Maté is a shared drink and, as such, has a big and widespread social role. The drink is traditionally served in gourds, which are often mounted in silver and are precious objects. The maté is sipped through a silver straw, then passed on to the next person.

To make maté, you first put a little cold water into your gourd, pack a couple of teaspoons of maté leaf into the water and mash it in. Top up with boiling water, sweeten to taste and sip. It's rude to slurp or to drink with the straw sticking out of the side of your mouth. Pass it around, but watch out for the gaucho with cold sores. When it's empty, pour on more boiling water. One fill of the gourd can make several cupfuls. You see bus drivers and long distance lorry drivers drinking maté to keep them awake and one side effect of this maté craze is the endless displays of fancy thermos flasks in every shop.

EMPANADAS

Another Argentinian favourite is the empanada.
Again, there is a great tradition with these little
pasties, which are about half the size of a regular
Cornish pasty. Typical of the Argentinians' appetite
is that empanadas are often served as a starter before
your meal. It's great – a pie as a starter! In some
places I have even seen empanadas served as an
amuse-bouche (you know, the poncy, free appetizer
that you are given before you order). What heroes.
It's a pie.

The most common filling is beef, usually with green
olives and hard-boiled egg. We had some lovely lamb
empanadas in Patagonia, but, in fact, if you can wrap
it in pastry and bake it, you can make it into an
empanada. A nice touch is that they crimp the edge of
the pastry in different ways to help identify different
empanadas. For example, beef ones may be crimped
closed with a fork, while chicken ones might have the
edge rolled over. Empanada creativity is endless.

DULCHE DE LECHE

Alongside a love of beef, the Argentinians have a rabid sweet tooth. This finds solace in dulche de leche, a sort of milk jam or caramelized milk. You find many different brands in the supermarket and everyone has their favourite. It's the Latin American kids' equivalent of Nutella. Eat it on its own or with ice cream, but please do try the recipe for the dulche de leche cheesecake in this book. It's a winner.

Well, don't cry for me, Argentina. Oh shut up, there's no need to blub because the food's great. It's a bit of a long way to go for supper, but dinner in Buenos Aires followed by a night in a tango club is definitely something to do before you die.

PRAWN CHUPE SERVES 4

Chupe is the South American equivalent of chowder, a thick hearty soup to get stuck to your tummy. It's great for a lunch or supper dish served with Arepas (see our recipe on page 102) or crusty bread smothered in butter. Ooh go on, forget your waistline for a while.

750ml chicken or fish stock

2 sticks of celery, thinly sliced
  (with leaves on if you can get them,
  so you can chuck them in as well)

1 carrot, thinly sliced

1 large tomato

3 tablespoons olive oil

1 large onion, finely chopped

1 red pepper, seeded and chopped

1 red chilli, seeded and chopped

4 cloves of garlic, crushed

700g floury potatoes,
  peeled and chopped into 1cm cubes

1 teaspoon turmeric

500g peeled raw king prawns

120g frozen peas

2 tablespoons double cream

a handful of fresh coriander

In a large saucepan with a lid, bring the stock to the boil and add the celery and carrot. Turn the heat down and simmer for 20 minutes to enrich the stock, then strain and set aside.

Remove the eye from the tomato, place in a bowl and pour over boiling water. Leave to stand for 10 to 15 seconds before draining. Peel away the skin and chop.

In a large frying pan, heat the oil over a medium heat, and cook the onion and red pepper for about 7 minutes until the onion is translucent. Add the chilli and the garlic and cook for a further 2 minutes, keeping them on the move in the pan with the help of a wooden spoon. Add the potato, tomato and turmeric to the frying pan, season with salt and black pepper and cook for a further 10 minutes, stirring all the time, to allow the tomato to break down and the potato to take on all the flavours.

Add the strained stock and potato mix to the large saucepan and bring to the boil. Cook gently for 10 minutes with the lid on, and then a further 10 minutes with the lid off, until the potatoes are cooked.

Add the prawns and peas and cook for a further 3 minutes. Remove from the heat and stir in the cream and fresh coriander. Don't worry about the thickness of the soup, chupe is supposed to be a thick and hearty meal.

Serve in warm bowls with arepas or buttered bread.

AREPAS MAKES ABOUT 10

Popular all over South America, these cornmeal scones, crisp on the outside and soft in the middle, are delicious served with our Chupe (see page 101). Alternatively, split and fill with a really nice melted cheese or stuff in some smoky bacon and pour maple syrup over the top for breakfast.

When buying the flour, ask for harina pan, a white cornmeal flour. You could use masa harina like we used in Mexico, but harina pan is a better bet. Don't use yellow cornmeal or you'll end up with an interesting polenta cake-vibe. It really is worth finding the right flour because arepas are fantastic.

1 teaspoon salt
375g harina pan flour
1 tablespoon Parmesan cheese
  (optional)
3 tablespoons corn oil

Mix the salt and Parmesan (if using) with the harina pan. Add 450 to 500ml cold water a little at a time, and blend to make a soft dough. Leave to rest for 20 minutes. It really is as simple as that.

Shape the dough into hamburger-sized rounds. Fry in the hot oil for 3 to 5 minutes each side until golden and crisp on the outside, but still soft in the middle. Split and serve with butter.

GAZPACHO SERVES 8

A classic, but still a good 'un. A summer soup for those hot, lazy South American evenings in Clapham or Hull. Or make this soup when your gas meter runs out and the giro hasn't arrived (come on, we've all been there) – no cooking involved.

3 large tomatoes
½ large cucumber
1 green pepper, very finely chopped
1 red pepper, very finely chopped
4 spring onions,
  very finely chopped
3 cloves of garlic, crushed
1 teaspoon fresh thyme leaves
1 teaspoon paprika
4 tablespoons olive oil
1 litre cold chicken stock

juice of 1 lime
2 tablespoons finely chopped
  fresh flat-leaf parsley
1 tablespoon red wine vinegar
1 litre tomato juice
salt crackers, to serve
8 radishes, sliced
1 avocado, cubed
a good bunch of fresh basil, torn
  by the hands of an Italian peasant

Remove the eye from the tomatoes, place in a bowl and pour over boiling water. Leave to stand for 10 to 15 seconds before draining. Peel away the skin, take out the seeds and very finely chop.

Peel the cucumber, scrape out the seeds and finely chop.

Place the tomato and cucumber in a bowl and add the green pepper, red pepper, spring onion, garlic, thyme, paprika, olive oil, chicken stock, lime juice, parsley, red wine vinegar and tomato juice.

Check the seasoning, and then place in the fridge for at least 4 hours to infuse all the flavours.

To serve, place a couple of broken salt crackers in the bottom of your serving bowl (like submerged croutons) and fill the bowl with soup. Top with sliced radish, a couple of cubes of avocado and some torn basil leaves and ladle out.

ONION AND RADISH SALAD

SERVES 4 AS A SIDE SALAD

We love onion salad in any form, but particularly with meat cooked over an Argentinian parrilla (BBQ). This little number is best avoided as a first-date supper salad, but if it's going to last, they won't mind how you smell.

2 large onions, sliced

5 tablespoons olive oil

2 tablespoons red wine vinegar

2 cloves of garlic, crushed

½ teaspoon chilli powder

6 large radishes, sliced, or 12 small

a good handful of chopped fresh parsley

a good handful of chopped fresh coriander

1 teaspoon sugar

Separate the onion slices into rings and place in a bowl. Cover with boiling water and leave for 15 minutes (this takes the heat and bitterness away from the onion).

Meanwhile, pour the olive oil and red wine vinegar into a salad bowl. Add the garlic, chilli powder, radish, parsley, coriander, sugar, salt and pepper to taste and mix well.

Drain the onion and plunge into cold water. Shake dry and add to the bowl with the other ingredients.

Leave for a couple of hours to infuse the flavours. Serve with a big steak and a glass of red.

AVOCADO AND GRAPEFRUIT SALAD

SERVES 4 AS A SIDE SALAD

This refreshing salad is great with meat, which is handy really as we've eaten a lot of the best beef Argentina has to offer. When you get fed up with potatoes and fancy a change, this is the one for you. Try it with a glass of red and a steak – could this be the grapefruit diet that people really want to eat?

2 pink grapefruits
2 avocadoes, skinned, stoned and cut
  into chunks (story of my life!)
1 tablespoon olive oil
a bag of rocket leaves

Peel the grapefruit, running a serrated knife down the sides of the fruit to take away the skin and pith and leave the flesh (make sure you have no pith because this white horror is really bitter). You should be left with a juicy, slippery ball. Carefully remove each segment over a bowl, collecting the juice because you will need this later.

Add the segments and the juice to the avocado chunks and mix in the olive oil. Add salt and pepper to taste and gently stir.

Put the rocket in the centre of a serving plate to form a bed, then get a handful of the avocado and grapefruit and place on the rocket. Spoon the juice over the salad and allow to trickle through the rocket leaves. Serve to all your really thin friends.

ESCABECHE SERVES 6 AS A STARTER

Escabeche, a dish of lightly pickled white fish, is great as a light starter or as part of a buffet. In Argentina, escabeche has evolved to include local herbs and vegetables (some people even add chopped hard-boiled egg, which we're not so keen on). Our version is light and flavoursome, but has enough tasty ingredients to stand out as an interesting dish on its own. The fish are first fried, so this recipe is good for people who are put off by raw fish.

1 red pepper, julienned
(cut into thin strips)

4 spring onions, finely chopped

1 red chilli, seeded and
finely chopped

2 cloves of garlic, crushed

finely grated zest of
1 unwaxed lemon

2 tablespoons chopped capers

3 tablespoons chopped black olives

6 cornichons (little gherkins),
thinly sliced

4 tablespoons olive oil

2 tablespoons sherry vinegar

a good handful of chopped
fresh coriander, stalks and all

500g thin, small white fish fillets,
such as sea bass, red mullet,
swordfish or bream, skinned

1 teaspoon salt

plain flour, for coating

2 tablespoons vegetable oil

In a mixing bowl, combine the red pepper, spring onion, chilli, garlic, lemon zest, capers, olives, cornichons, olive oil, sherry vinegar and coriander.

Trim the fish fillets so they are nice and tidy. Sprinkle on the salt and leave for 1 hour to draw out any excess moisture from the fish. Then, with kitchen roll, blot the fish until it is really dry.

In a shallow dish, coat the fish fillets in the flour.

In a large frying pan, heat the vegetable oil over a medium heat until it is hot. Shake off the excess flour from the fish and fry the fillets for about 2 minutes each side until they are golden but not burnt.

Place the fish on a platter and spoon over the salad mix, making sure all the juices go on as well (as the fish cools, it will take in all the wonderful flavours). Leave in the refrigerator for at least an hour before serving. Lovely with a glass of chilled dry white wine.

SCALLOPINI BUENOS AIRES   SERVES 4

Taken from the shores of Italy, this recipe is clearly here due to the huge influx of Italians seeking new lives and fortunes in this wonderful country in the nineteenth century. Argentina is a long way on a flight, so can you imagine the courage it would have taken to sail halfway across the world?

500g fillet steak

2 eggs

3 cloves of garlic, crushed

2 teaspoons dried parsley

1 teaspoon dried oregano

½ teaspoon salt

½ teaspoon ground black pepper

½ teaspoon chilli powder

250g breadcrumbs, dried and toasted (make your own, they're better)

3 tablespoons vegetable oil

1 tablespoon butter

lemon wedges, for serving

Slice the beef really thin and beat to a beer-mat thickness by placing the slices in clingfilm and hitting with a rolling pin.

Crack your eggs into a bowl and beat. Add the garlic, dried parsley, oregano, salt, black pepper and chilli powder and mix well.

Add the thin slices of steak, one by one, to the egg mixture, making sure all of each slice is covered. Repeat the process until all the slices are sitting in the egg mixture. Leave to marinate for an hour in the fridge.

Place the breadcrumbs in a bowl. (To make your own toasted breadcrumbs, remove the crusts from a stale, white loaf of bread; cut the loaf into chunks and put the chunks into a blender or food processor, then pulse until they are reduced to crumbs. Place the crumbs on a baking tray and put into the oven (preheated to 180°C) for 5 to 10 minutes or until pale golden brown and lightly crispy.)

In a frying pan, heat the oil and butter over a medium heat. Remove the slices of steak from the marinade and, one at a time, dip into the breadcrumbs, making sure each slice is completely covered in crumbs (press the crumbs into the steak with your hands). Fry no more than two slices at a time. Cook for about 3 minutes on each side until golden.

Serve immediately with lemon wedges.

BEEF EMPANADAS   MAKES ABOUT 6

You find empanadas everywhere in South America. The most common empanada is the beef one, sometimes combined with almonds or fruit like peaches and pears, although chicken, cheese and ham, creamed corn and tuna are aplenty. Empanadas can be made in bulk and frozen; just take them out of the freezer about 3 hours before you need them.

for the pastry

450g plain flour

2 teaspoons baking powder

1 teaspoon salt

60g lard or vegetable shortening

60g butter

for the filling

2 tablespoons olive oil

½ beef stock cube, crumbled

400g fillet steak (or sirloin
  if you're skint), finely chopped

1 onion, finely chopped

1 small green pepper, finely chopped

3 cloves of garlic, crushed

3 tablespoons red wine

½ teaspoon ground cumin

½ teaspoon paprika

½ teaspoon chilli powder

12 pimento-stuffed green olives,
  chopped

1 teaspoon salt

½ teaspoon ground black pepper

1 egg, beaten

First make the pastry. In a mixing bowl, mix together the flour, baking powder and salt. Cut the lard and butter into sugar-cube-sized chunks and add to the flour, rubbing the fat into the flour until it becomes crumblike. Add enough cold water to make a soft dough (approximately 75–100ml). Set aside in the fridge to rest for an hour.

While the pastry is chilling out, make the filling. In a large frying pan, heat 1 tablespoon of the oil over a medium to high heat and sprinkle in the stock cube. Fry for 30 seconds, stirring continuously. Add the beef and fry for 2 minutes until brown (don't overcook good meat). Set this to one side.

Heat the remaining tablespoon of olive oil in the frying pan over a medium heat, add the onion and green pepper and fry for about 3 minutes until soft. Add the garlic and fry for a further minute. Add the wine, cumin, paprika, chilli powder, olives and the salt and pepper. Fry for a further minute, stirring continuously. Return the meat and juices to the pan and mix well. Set aside to go cold.

Preheat the oven to 180°C. Take the pastry out of the refrigerator and, on a well-floured surface, roll out to a thin sheet. Using a saucer as a template, cut out discs of pastry.

On one half of each circle, place a tablespoonful of the filling. Brush the edge with egg, fold over and crimp the edges together to make a flat pasty. Argentinian cooks get creative by having different styles of crimped edges so that you can identify the filling.

Brush with more egg and place on a greased baking tray. Bake for about 20 minutes or until golden. These are delicious eaten hot or cold.

KIDNEYS IN SHERRY SAUCE
WITH BUTTER POTATOES
SERVES 2 AS A MAIN DISH OR 4 AS A STARTER

In Argentina it's not all about eating steak. A lot of offal is also cooked on the parrilla (BBQ) and people love sweetbreads marinated in a little lemon, braised chicken hearts and chargrilled kidneys. People in the UK can be a bit funny about eating offal, but one thing that most people love is kidneys, especially comfy steak and kidney pies. This dish of lovely herby kidneys cooked in a traditional sherry sauce is mixed with buttery potatoes to give a complete meal.

2 large potatoes
2 tablespoons olive oil
1 onion, finely chopped
1 stick of celery, finely chopped
1 large carrot, finely chopped
2 cloves of garlic, crushed
2 teaspoons fresh thyme leaves

500g lamb's kidneys, halved and cored (i.e. cut out the white, hard, fatty bit in the middle)
4 tablespoons dry sherry
50g butter
2 teaspoons crème fraîche
1 tablespoon fresh flat-leaf parsley, finely chopped

First, cook the whole potatoes with their skins on in a big pan of boiling water for about 20 minutes until cooked through (test with a skewer). Leave to cool, then peel, chop into 1cm cubes and set aside.

In a large frying pan, heat the olive oil and fry the onion, celery and carrot for about 5 minutes over a low heat until the onion is translucent. Add the garlic, stir and cook for another minute.

Add the thyme and kidneys and fry for a couple of minutes until the kidneys start to brown. Pour in the sherry and simmer gently for another 3 minutes to cook the kidneys through and to make the sauce a little less liquid. Set aside for a couple of minutes to rest while you get the potatoes ready.

Heat the butter in another frying pan and toss the cold potato cubes for 8 to 10 minutes until they start to take on some colour. Season to taste.

Fold in the kidneys and warm through. Finish off by checking the seasoning and stirring in the crème fraîche and the parsley. This is a dish that is anything but offal – it's blooming great!

PORK RAVIOLI WITH SAGE BUTTER

SERVES 8 AS A STARTER OR 4 AS A MAIN COURSE

Argentinian cooks have a happy habit of taking the best of Italian, French and most other European cuisines, mixing

them together and calling it their own. A good thing if you ask us. This recipe is inspired by a pumpkin ravioli served with sage butter we ate while in Buenos Aires. We have replaced the pumpkin with a tasty, simple pork filling. Give it a go, it's a great eat.

for the ravioli pasta
250g strong plain flour
4 small eggs
2 tablespoons olive oil

for the filling
1 tablespoon olive oil
1 onion, finely chopped
2 cloves of garlic, crushed
300g minced pork
1 teaspoon fresh thyme leaves
3 tablespoons white wine
1 egg, beaten

for the sage butter
a handful of fresh sage leaves
100g unsalted butter
Parmesan cheese, to serve

To make the pasta, put the flour, eggs and olive oil into a bowl and beat with a wooden spoon (or put into a food processor with a dough blade and whizz) until a dough ball forms. Set aside to rest in the fridge for at least 1 hour.

To make the filling, heat the olive oil in a frying pan over a medium heat, add the onion and fry until translucent. This should take about 10 to 15 minutes. Add the garlic and cook for another 2 minutes. Add the pork and thyme and cook for 2 minutes more to lightly brown the pork. Pour in the white wine and cook for a final 2 minutes until the alcohol evaporates. Add salt and pepper to taste and set aside to cool.

To form the ravioli, roll out your pasta on a very well floured surface as thin as you dare. Cut into discs with a pastry cutter or rim of a glass or just cut into squares if you prefer. As long as they are all the same size, it really doesn't matter what you do.

Once you have your preferred shapes, take a teaspoon of the filling and place in the centre of each one. The bigger your ravioli shape, the more filling you will need. However, the most important thing is not to overfill them.

Brush around the edge of each of the ravioli with the beaten egg and fold to seal in the filling, crimping the edge. Carefully drop the ravioli into a big pan of gently simmering water (make sure it has lots of water, the more water the better) and cook for about 3 to 5 minutes.

To make the sage butter, take the sage leaves in your hand and give them a tight squeeze so you bruise the leaves. Add to a warm, NOT HOT, saucepan and leave for 30 seconds (this little tip brings out the oil in the sage leaves). Add the butter and allow to melt over a very low heat. It is important that the butter does not bubble in the pan, but heats slowly to allow the sage leaves time to flavour it.

To serve, sprinkle the ravioli with ground black pepper and pour over your warm sage butter. Sprinkle with Parmesan if you like.

FISH WITH A CHORIZO CRUST

SERVES 4

We've cooked this dish at numerous dinner parties because it's really easy to feed lots of guests with and people love it. Place your fish in a roasting tin, then 20 minutes before you want everyone to eat, bung it in the oven and Bob's your uncle, you've cooked a gobsmacker!

4 meaty white fish fillets (such as cod, haddock, monkfish or halibut)
juice of ½ lime
150g dry white bread, crusts removed
250g cured chorizo sausage, skinned and chopped into big chunks
2 cloves of garlic, chopped

zest of 1 unwaxed lime
2 tablespoons fresh flat-leaf parsley, chopped
2 tablespoons Parmesan cheese, grated
½ teaspoon ground black pepper
50g butter
lime wedges, to serve

Preheat the oven to 180°C.

Take the fish portions and pour over the lime juice. Leave for half an hour while you prepare the crust.

Cut the bread into chunks, place in a roasting tin and arrange the chorizo on top. Cook in the oven for 15 minutes, allowing the bread to dry out. As the heat increases, the fat from the sausage will run into your bread chunks – this is a good thing. Remove from the oven and leave to cool.

Once cool, place the bread and sausage into a blender or food processor and blitz to crumbs. Add the garlic, lime zest, parsley, Parmesan and pepper and blitz together to combine the ingredients.

In a roasting tin, place the fish skin-side down and press on a good thick layer of the chorizo crust. Cut the butter into small cubes and dot over the crust. Tightly seal the roasting tin with foil and bake for 15 to 20 minutes. Serve with chips or new potatoes and a rocket salad. Don't forget your lime wedges.

CHORIZO AND BRANDY CHICKEN   SERVES 4

Argentinian food has loads of Spanish and European influences and chorizo and Spanish cheeses abound in South America. This is a lovely way of cooking chicken, poaching it first in a fragrant broth so the chicken remains juicy, then finishing it off in the oven with a rich chorizo and brandy sauce. It's also a good opportunity to use up that Fundador Spanish brandy that you brought back from your hols – it works a treat.

2 tablespoons vegetable oil

1 chicken, jointed (get your butcher to do this or buy chicken portions)

570ml chicken stock

1 onion, peeled and quartered

2 cloves

1 large carrot, halved

1 stick of celery, halved

2 bay leaves

a couple of sprigs of fresh thyme

1 teaspoon smoked paprika

4 cloves of garlic, skin on but slightly bruised (i.e. gently bashed with a rolling pin or a small saucepan)

for the sauce

1 tablespoon plain flour

1 tablespoon unsalted butter

4 tablespoons brandy

100g cured chorizo sausage, finely chopped

100g Spanish Manchego cheese, grated (Parmesan will do)

In a frying pan, heat the oil over a medium heat and brown the chicken portions all over for about 5 or 6 minutes.

In a large saucepan, bring the stock to the boil. Stud one of the onion quarters with the two cloves and add all the onion to the pan with the chicken, carrot, celery, bay leaves, thyme, paprika and garlic. Simmer very gently, uncovered, for 30 minutes, just until the chicken starts to fall apart. Remove the chicken and place in a roasting tin. Strain the stock and set aside. Preheat the oven to 180°C.

Next, make the sauce. In a saucepan, bring the reserved stock to the boil and simmer until the liquid has reduced by half.

In a bowl, mash the flour and butter together into a paste (this, in chef terms, is a **beurre manié**). Whisk this paste into the stock along with the brandy and simmer for 3 to 4 minutes to make a thickened sauce. Add the chorizo and season to taste. Pour this sauce over the chicken and sprinkle over the grated cheese. Bake for 10 to 15 minutes until brown. This is nice served with jacket potatoes and green beans.

SOUTH AMERICAN CHILLI CON CARNE

SERVES 6 GREEDY GAUCHOS

Black beans are a South American staple and I think they have more flavour than kidney beans. The chilli is a great dark, deep colour that will warm the cockles of your heart. This will taste even better the next day, so don't worry about leftovers.

250g black beans, soaked overnight
3 tablespoons olive oil
2 good-quality beef stock cubes
500g minced beef
2 onions, sliced
1 green pepper, chopped
1 red pepper, chopped
6 cloves of garlic, crushed
2 red chillies, seeded and chopped
2 green chillies, seeded and chopped
2 x 400g tins of plum tomatoes

1 tablespoon tomato purée
2 teaspoons hot paprika
1 teaspoon ground cumin
1 teaspoon salt
1 teaspoon ground black pepper
1 teaspoon sugar
2 bay leaves
Tabasco sauce, to taste.
a good handful of chopped fresh flat-leaf parsley

In a large pan of unsalted boiling water, simmer the black beans for about 45 minutes until soft. Test by pinching one between your fingers to see if it's soft. Drain and set aside.

In a large saucepan, heat up the oil over a medium heat and crumble in the stock cube. Fry until the stock cube dissolves and bubbles. Add the mince and fry for a couple of minutes until browned. With a perforated spoon, remove the meat and set aside. In the same pan and in the leftover oil and meat juices, gently cook the onion and green and red pepper for 4 to 5 minutes until the onion is translucent. Add the garlic and the red and green chilli and cook for a further 2 minutes.

Return the meat to the pan. Add the beans, tomatoes, tomato purée, paprika, cumin, salt, black pepper, sugar and the bay leaves. Cover and simmer ever so gently, over a low heat, for at least 2 hours.

Taste and adjust the seasoning. Now, it's time to use the Tabasco sauce as a heat adjuster. If you want a bit more heat, add the Tabasco until you get the chilli as hot as you like it and, as Marilyn Monroe says, some do like it hot . . . When you're happy, stir in the handful of parsley. By the way, at the end of the meal if you eat a sprig of parsley, it will take away the smell of garlic and will also stop you being so windy after all the beans.

PATAGONIAN LAMB ADOBE SERVES 4

There is a huge Welsh influence in Patagonia and they farm their sheep with the same skill and expertise they used in the hills and valleys of Wales before they left their homeland for a new life in Argentina. We love lamb, be it Cumbrian salt marsh, Northumbrian Blackface or Patagonian. Whichever you use, keep it real and buy it from your butcher. The quality and taste will be better.

20g dried porcini mushrooms

1 tablespoon olive oil

2 teaspoons red wine vinegar

1 onion, very finely chopped

3 cloves of garlic, crushed

1 teaspoon finely chopped fresh rosemary

1 tablespoon finely chopped fresh parsley

1 teaspoon dried oregano

1 teaspoon sugar

½ teaspoon salt

½ teaspoon ground black pepper

2 whole lamb loin fillets (the juicy bit of the chop, not the neck fillet – ask your butcher, he'll know)

250g thin streaky bacon or pancetta

Preheat the oven to 200°C.

In a bowl of hot water, soak the porcini mushrooms for about 20 minutes, then chop and mash into a paste.

In a bowl, blender or small food processor, put the oil, vinegar, onion, garlic, rosemary, parsley, oregano, sugar, mushrooms, salt and pepper. Mash or blend all the ingredients together to form a paste (adobe).

Trim your loin fillets of any nasty bits.

On a chopping board, place the bacon rashers side by side to form a sheet. Place one of the fillets over half the rasher ends so you're ready to roll it up. Take half the adobe paste and spread evenly over the top of the fillet, then roll the fillet, wrapping it up in the bacon sheet. Repeat the process with the second fillet.

Place the two fillets in a roasting tin, making sure the rasher ends are tucked in under the lamb on the bottom of the tin. Cook for 20 minutes if you like it medium, 15 minutes if you like it pink and 25 minutes if you like it well done.

Remove from the oven and allow to rest for 5 to 10 minutes. Serve with mash and root vegetables.

GAUCHOS' SAUSAGES WITH LENTILS

SERVES 4

Get your poncho, you've pulled. Well, you will have if you cook this wonderful, comforting one-pot dish on your first date. Argentina has really tasty sausages, but don't forget the great British banger. This is fantastic with Cumberland sausages, but you can use whatever good English sausages you can find. The chorizo is an optional extra that gives the stew a great colour and some extra zip.

250g lentils
  (green or orange, it's up to you)
1 tablespoon olive oil
500g good sausages
1 red pepper, seeded and
  cut into strips
1 onion, finely chopped
2 sticks of celery, chopped
2 ripe tomatoes, chopped

3 cloves of garlic, crushed
1 butternut squash,
  peeled and cubed
2 bay leaves
a big sprig of fresh thyme
100g chorizo sausage, chopped
50g long-grain rice, rinsed in
  cold water
290ml chicken stock

Cook the lentils in a pan of boiling water until soft (see the instructions on the back of the packet for the times). A good tip is never to salt the water that you are going to cook the lentils in because this will make them go hard. Drain and set aside.

In a large saucepan, heat the oil, prick and then brown your sausages for 3 to 4 minutes over a medium heat, giving them a shake in the pan from time to time. Set aside.

In the same saucepan, add the pepper and onion to the sausage fat and oil in the pan and cook for 4 to 5 minutes over a medium heat until the onions become translucent. Add the celery, tomato, garlic, squash, bay leaves and thyme and cook for a further 2 minutes.

Add the sausages, chorizo, lentils and rice, give it a good stir and pour over the stock. Simmer gently for 20 to 30 minutes with the lid off until the rice and squash are cooked and the lentils and sausages are tender. Season to taste.

This is a good hearty winter dish, great served with some warm crusty bread and butter.

SPICED PORK WITH RUM   SERVES 4

Traditionally this is cooked on a BBQ and, to our minds, this is the best thing to do (well, it would be, wouldn't it?). However, you can cook it in the oven and the result will be fine.

2 pork fillets
2 tablespoons olive oil

for the marinade
3 cloves of garlic
2 tablespoons balsamic vinegar
1 teaspoon dried thyme
1 teaspoon dried sage
½ teaspoon mixed spice
2 teaspoons curry powder
1 tablespoon muscovado sugar

4 tablespoons rum
½ teaspoon salt
½ teaspoon pepper

for the sauce
250ml chicken stock
1 tablespoon tomato purée
1 tablespoon demerara sugar
Tabasco sauce, to taste
2 tablespoons butter
1 tablespoon chopped fresh parsley

To make the marinade, put all the ingredients into a blender and blend until smooth. It couldn't be easier.

In order to massage the marinade into your meat, you need to make a hole through the length of your pork fillet. The best way to do this is to take the handle of a wooden spoon and push it through the length of each piece of pork to make a hole. Now, practise your massage skills by gradually pouring the marinade into the hole and working it into the meat. Use the marinade that will run out of the hole to rub the outside of the meat. Place the pork in a roasting tin and refrigerate for at least a couple of hours or preferably overnight (the longer the better) to marinate.

Preheat the oven to 180°C.

Now take your fillets, still in the roasting tin, and add the olive oil (to stop them sticking). Cook (or put straight on to the barbie) for about 25 minutes. Remove from the oven and the tin and set aside to rest. Meanwhile, prepare the sauce.

Place your roasting tin on top of the stove and, over a slow flame, deglaze the tin with the chicken stock, scraping up all those lovely juicy bits. Add the tomato purée, sugar and Tabasco sauce and bring to the boil. Boil for 5 minutes until the sauce is a little less liquid. Just before serving, whisk in the butter and parsley. Serve the sauce alongside the carved pork. Eat with mashed potatoes and honey-glazed carrots.

ARGENTINE PORK AND RICE

SERVES 4 HUNGRY BOYS

This is traditional comfort food in Argentina and everyone loves it. Each family has its own recipe and granny's is always best. Our recipe takes all the best of granny's secrets to make a great dish for the long winter nights. A fantastic one-pot wonder.

a pinch of saffron

2 bay leaves

1 litre chicken stock

3 tablespoons olive oil

500g boneless pork shoulder, trimmed and cut into chunks

1 onion, sliced

3 cloves of garlic, crushed

2 teaspoons dried sage

300g long-grain rice

½ teaspoon salt

½ teaspoon ground black pepper (you can adjust the seasoning to taste)

100g pimentos (roasted peppers in a jar), cut into strips

50g roasted unsalted peanuts, roughly chopped

Soak the saffron and bay leaves in hot stock and leave to infuse for 5 minutes.

In a casserole dish with a lid, heat the oil over a medium heat and brown the pork for 5 to 6 minutes, then remove and set aside.

In the pork dripping and olive oil, brown your onion for 3 to 4 minutes, then add the garlic and sage and cook for a further 2 minutes. Add the rice and coat with the oily onion and garlic juices (much the same as you would do for a risotto). Cook for a minute, stirring continuously.

Add the set-aside pork in a layer on top of the rice and season with the salt and pepper.

Pour on the stock with the saffron and bay leaves. DO NOT STIR (this may seem strange, but you want the pork flavours to cook down into the rice). Bring to the boil.

You now have a choice of simmering on the stovetop over a gentle heat for 30 minutes or cooking in a 160°C oven for 30 minutes.

When cooked, leave to rest for 5 minutes, then fluff up the rice and transfer to a serving dish. Garnish with the pimento slices and chopped peanuts. Serve with a hearty salad.

SPICY MASHED POTATOES   SERVES 4

Mash goes great with meat dishes and in Argentina they are not afraid to experiment. One of our favourites is this pure picante, a buttery, spicy mashed potato with a chilli sauce. The chilli sauce is great, so make double and keep some in the fridge. Try this with our spiced pork with rum . . . **ai carumba**!

1.5kg floury potatoes
(good mashers like King Edwards,
Maris Piper or Desirée)
1 bay leaf
50ml milk
50g butter

for the chilli sauce
5 hot red chillies,
seeded and chopped
3 cloves of garlic
2 tablespoons olive oil
¼ teaspoon salt

Peel the potatoes and cook them in a pan of lightly salted boiling water with the bay leaf for 15 to 20 minutes or until soft. Drain and discard the bay leaf.

Meanwhile, make the chilli sauce. In a blender, blitz the chillies, garlic, oil and salt with 1 tablespoon hot water. Set aside.

Mash the potatoes with the milk and butter into a purée with a potato masher or ricer. Season to taste.

Mix the chilli sauce into the mash (depending on the strength of the chillies and how hot you like it, about a teaspoonful should be plenty). Any extra sauce can be kept under a little oil in the fridge for a couple of weeks and used at a later date.

Ooh, it's a good one. Bangers and mash will never be the same.

JULIE'S DULCHE DE LECHE CHEESECAKE

MAKES 8 GOOD-SIZED SLICES

This is a great recipe given to us by Julie, a dainty blonde powerhouse of a woman who we met at her estancia (ranch) while we were learning to be gauchos. It is fantastic and her family all rallied round to say that this was one of their favourites. It's dead simple and, like all solid family favourites, it's worth sharing. Thanks, Julie.

400g Oreo cookies (or Hobnobs)
150g melted unsalted butter
750g cream cheese
  (such as Philadelphia)
½ teaspoon vanilla extract

600g dulche de leche, bought or
  made from 2 tins of condensed
  milk (see our recipe opposite)
2 eggs
2 tablespoons cornflour

Preheat the oven to 140ºC.

Put the Oreo cookies or Hobnobs in a plastic bag and bash them into crumbs with a rolling pin.

Transfer the biscuits from the bag into a bowl, pour over the melted butter and mix together well. Pile into a well-buttered 23cm springform tin (at least 7cm deep) and spread evenly, pressing it down to form a solid, even layer. This is your biscuit base (with Oreo cookies, this will resemble a tarmac road!). Chill for half an hour or so while you make the topping.

Put the cream cheese in a large mixing bowl, beat in your vanilla and the dulche de leche, and then add the eggs, one at a time, beating them in as you go. Finally, beat in the cornflour and pour the mixture on top of the biscuit base.

Bake for 1 hour 30 minutes. When cool, remove from the tin and serve. This is very rich, but funnily enough it doesn't seem too sweet – it is sweet in a sort of grown-up way. Nice served with a fresh fruit coulis (a fruit purée to you and me).

DULCHE DE LECHE

A true Argentinian creation, dulche de leche, 'sweet milk', is used as a filling or topping for numerous desserts and can be spread on bread much the same way as French kids eat Nutella. Once made, you can keep it in a jar for months, so it is worth making three or four batches (i.e. cans) at the same time. It's great for filling pancakes and such a good standby for ice cream. Below is the quick, everyday way to make dulche de leche. If you don't want to go to the hassle of making it, it is available at most big supermarkets.

1 can of condensed milk!

Place the unopened can of condensed milk in a saucepan of gently boiling water. MAKE SURE THE CAN IS COVERED WITH WATER.

Simmer for 3 hours. UNDER NO CIRCUMSTANCES MUST THE PAN BOIL DRY BECAUSE IF IT IS NOT FULLY SUBMERGED IN THE WATER, THE CAN WILL EXPLODE AND DESTROY THE KITCHEN. YOU HAVE BEEN WARNED.

Carefully lift the hot can from the water and leave to cool completely (if you open the can when hot, the contents will spurt out and could cause serious burns).

Empty the can into a jar and the dulche de leche is now ready for use.

In South America, housewives often throw in an unopened can of condensed milk while boiling beans, so they cook their beans and create pudding at the same time.

PINEAPPLE CRÈME CARAMEL   SERVES 4

A real family pudding. Fresh pineapple is such a wonderful fruit and when crossed with the ever-popular crème caramel, it makes a top pudding. No cream or ice cream required – lovely.

350g fresh pineapple,
  peeled and chopped
150g caster sugar
4 eggs, very lightly beaten
½ teaspoon vanilla extract

for the caramel
80g caster sugar
juice of 1 lime

Put the pineapple in a blender and purée until smooth. Scrape the purée into a pan and add the sugar. Cook over a medium heat for 5 minutes to reduce the liquid by a third. The texture should be thick, but not solid. If it looks dodgy, add a bit of water (no one will know, honest). Put the mixture in a bowl and set aside to cool.

Now make the caramel. Melt the sugar in a pan over a medium heat and, as it starts to caramelize at the edges, shake the pan but do not stir; keep your eye on it as it can turn very quickly. After about 5 to 10 minutes, you should have a golden coloured liquid. Add the lime juice to taste (this will also stop it burning). Put a puddle of caramel into 4 ramekins.

Preheat the oven to 180°C.

Mix the beaten eggs with the vanilla and the cold pineapple purée gently and pour into the ramekins over the caramel. Place the ramekins in a roasting tin and pour in boiling water so the water reaches a centimetre below the top of the ramekins. Cover with foil.

Cook for 45 minutes until set, then allow to cool. Just before serving, turn out on to dessert plates and admire the mounds of wobbling loveliness in their sea of sauce.

TANDIL LEMON CAKE
WITH A CHERRY TOPPING SERVES 8-10

We discovered this great cake in a town called Tandil while travelling south through Argentina.

100g unsalted butter
 (at room temperature)
225g caster sugar
3 eggs, separated
1 tablespoon lemon zest
350g plain flour
2 teaspoons baking powder
1 teaspoon ground cinnamon
a pinch of salt
250ml whole milk

for the fruit topping
300g tinned or bottled sweet dark
 cherries in syrup
1 tablespoon cornflour
2 tablespoons lemon juice
2 tablespoons cherry brandy

Preheat the oven to 180°C. Butter the inside of a 23cm springform tin and line with buttered parchment paper.

In a food processor or with a wooden spoon, beat the butter and sugar until light and fluffy, then beat in the egg yolks, one at a time. Add the lemon zest.

Mix the flour, baking powder, cinnamon and salt together in a bowl and add to the butter and sugar mixture. Beat together to form crumbs. Pour in the milk gradually and mix to form a heavy batter.

In another bowl, beat the egg whites until they form soft peaks, then fold carefully into the cake mixture.

Pour the cake mixture into the cake tin and bake for 30 to 50 minutes or until a skewer inserted into the centre can be removed cleanly. Set aside to cool.

For the topping, drain the cherries and reserve a cup of the syrup. Place the reserved syrup in a saucepan and bring to the boil, and then reduce the heat to a simmer for 5 minutes. Mix the cornflour with the lemon juice and add to the syrup, stirring constantly. When the syrup is thick after 1 to 2 minutes, remove from the heat and add the cherry brandy. Set aside to cool.

Add a layer of cherries to the warm cake, then pour over the syrup. Leave to cool completely before serving with a big dollop of ice cream or clotted cream.

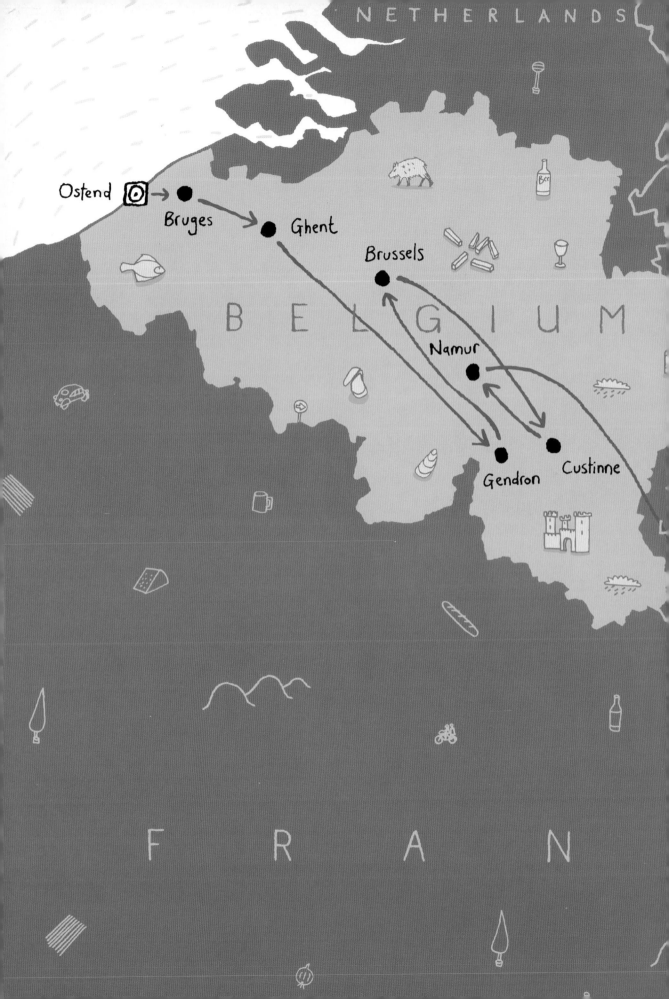

BELGIUM

Strasbourg

Sigolsheim

DAVE: Belgium is a funny one. Just mention of its name seems to bring a smile to people's faces. Look it up on the internet and bizarrely you'll find there are websites devoted to listing famous Belgians. This is, of course, because of the game where you try to name five famous Belgian people, but there is more to the country than Jean-Claude van Damme, Plastic Bertrand, Tintin and – you know, what are their names? – those tennis players. See, it's not easy.

Collectively we don't seem to know much about Belgium, but there is so much more to it than you might think. When you first arrive, all you see is sleepy farmland (a bit like a slightly dreary Kent) and an urban mess of cities the same as any others in northern Europe. But look a little closer and you realize that the place is madder than a host of hobbits, and happily so – honestly, a Finch Warble Counting Championship, I ask you! The food is amazing; the countryside varies from a great coastline to the beautiful Ardennes mountains and forests; and there is incredible architecture and moments of rare beauty in the cities.

'Dave can navigate through the air and at sea, but on land he has a problem with his left and right.' Si

BIKING

SI: The bikes of choice for Belgium were a couple of Moto Guzzi lovelies: a Breva and the new Griso, two really ace bikes from those nice people at Guzzi. On the styling front, the Griso has the edge. It's a work of art. That bike turns heads quicker than a naked supermodel. The power delivery was also much better on the Griso.

We visited Belgium in December when it was cold and wet. One great thing about the country is that you can get around in no time – partly because it's pretty damn flat. We went from Ostend to Bruges to Ghent to Brussels to the Ardennes without breaking a sweat, but we still got soaked. Cold weather saps your energy, your concentration falls away and fatigue soon takes over. It is therefore imperative that you do three things. Wear good windproof, waterproof gear; wear layers underneath your outer jacket; and stop regularly to have a break. Dave and I found that you really don't realize how tired you are until you stop and get off the bike. But, if you do wear good gear, there is nothing better than riding in the winter. We love it, and the challenge of the road conditions sharpens up your road craft no end.

Navigating in the freezing cold and rain can be a pain in the proverbial. Dave, however, has come up with a solution – a GPS designed for a bike. Now, Dave can navigate through the air and at sea, but on land he has a problem with his left and right and the phrase, 'The other left,' sprang out of my mouth with alarming regularity. Despite this, Dave's GPS was a godsend.

I thought I might have a bit of trouble writing about riding a bike in Belgium. Nowt ever happens, or so I thought. The roads are good, places are well signposted and all seems to be safe and quite pleasant. But that's Belgium, the façade hides what lies beneath.

> '**Surrealism was in many ways born in Belgium, as indeed, in a way, was I. My Mam and Dad met on a coach trip to Ostend and, after a massive amount of Belgian beer, chips and Northern passion, I popped out some time later.**' DAVE

SURREALISM IN OSTEND

SI: Ostend is a surprise. We roared off the boat expecting the usual North Sea ferry town ugliness, but instead we found a prosperous and pretty town full of art and fancy shops and great seafood.

DAVE: Surrealist art is all about taking ordinary, mundane objects and putting them into extraordinary, dreamlike situations to show us what an odd world we would live in if it was just a bit mixed up. Surrealism was in many ways born in Belgium, as indeed, in a way, was I. My Mam and Dad met on a coach trip to Ostend and, after a massive amount of Belgian beer, chips and Northern passion, I popped out some time later. The artist James Ensor also made a sudden appearance in Ostend, born here in 1860 (quite possibly also in a blaze of chips and beer). We've all heard of Magritte, the king of surrealism and one of Belgium's greatest contributions to world culture, but in Belgium, James Ensor is a household name and seen as the father of surrealism.

James Ensor's work is just fantastic. Visiting his house near the seafront in Ostend, we found out that his parents ran a curio shop on the ground floor where they sold Victorian oddities like stuffed 'mermaids' and dried seahorses. This unusual upbringing, combined with the colourful characters who visited the seaside, influenced Ensor's work.

You wouldn't have thought that this mild-looking old greybeard had a mind writhing with unholy visions, until you enter his house and walk bang into three leering mermen trying to get at you from behind their glass case. Then you go upstairs and find a wizened puppet with Ensor's wife's face on it, presiding over a gargoyle-strewn Victorian drawing room made for holding séances. So what could we do but ask her to reveal to us one of the Great Secrets of the Universe?

'Where can two foodie bikers find the best chips in the world?'

And the answer she gave us was 'In Belgium! In Bruges! In the main square!'

IN SEARCH OF CHIPS AND BEER IN BRUGES

SI: So off we went. Bruges is about half an hour by motorbike from Ostend, so by the time you take your first look at the city you are only halfway soaked, but completely stunned. It's a really beautiful little place, all medieval spires and turrets, canals and narrow cobbled streets. Not to mention the great chips! We looked at each other and agreed, a man could live in Bruges and never want to wander again. Part of that's the one-way system of course. Without a GPS like us, the average Belgian is forced to stay in this lovely town, eat the great local food and drink the three hundred local beers . . . hang about, let's scrap our GPS right now!

Keen as always to blend in, we set up a stall at the famous Bruges fish market, the medieval Vismarkt, to try our hand at cooking one of Belgium's specialities: mussels, chips and mayonnaise. And this is where the locals really brought home to us how deeply chips with mayonnaise is part of the national psyche. A crowd gathered, clustering around ever closer as we began laying out the fruits of our labours, baying for a chance to test our chips and mayonnaise. Even the neighbouring fishmongers dropped what they were doing and came over to try our wares.

Talk about bringing coals to Newcastle. Every single man and woman had an opinion: more lemon, less egg, wrong chip fat, different type of salt and so on. Grudgingly, a local chef, a couple of sheets to the wind on Bruges beer (and it wasn't even eleven in the morning) gave us an eight out of ten. It was getting ugly though – time to leave, with or without our trusty GPS.

> 'Bruges may have the best chips in Belgium, but it is also beer heaven.' DAVE

DAVE: Bruges may have the best chips in Belgium, but it is also beer heaven and two must-see places are a bar called Brugs Beertje, whose logo is a pissed-up teddy bear, and Den Dyver, a restaurant that specializes in fine dishes cooked with beer. Brugs Beertje is the bar of Daisy Claeys, a professor of beer, and it is warm and comfortable, just like her. She loves her beer and talking to her you realize just what a world and culture you are getting involved in. She chooses you a beer she knows you will like and her beer snacks are great: Flemish cheese and ham and slabs of rough, tasty Ardennes pâté. When I asked Daisy if she could choose one beer to drink for the rest of her life, with the exclusion of any others, she was unable to answer, explaining, 'There are different beers for different times and moods. It's not possible to give an answer. No! I can't.' A night in Brugs Beertje is definitely one of those things to do before you die.

Filip Vandenbussche, a member of the family who run the Den Dyver restaurant, is equally passionate about Belgian beer, but his approach is different. Filip has worked in Michelin-starred restaurants in Belgium and he applies this knowledge to the restaurant, starting with beer as his foundation. The food is very fine, cooked not in the traditional beef-and-beer stew way, but with beer 'sauces' carefully chosen to match the dish. The dry, light beers work really well with fish, and Filip cooked a wonderful rich, dark beer sauce for some wild boar he served while we were there. As the meal progresses, the beer used in the dishes is beautifully served in wine glasses so it can be sipped and savoured as you eat. The food here is divine. Belgian chocolate mousse served with a fruit beer reduction, anyone?

WATERZOOI
AND TRAMS IN GHENT

SI: Half an hour away from Bruges, Ghent's got much the same loveliness. There's a big, black medieval castle bang in the centre of town and more canals than you can shake a piston ring at. It might rain a bit, though. Might even rain hard. We bikers laugh at silly things like the weather, but the crew huddled under their umbrellas until the gale blew them all inside out and they missed the shot they were trying to get of us roaring by chased by a picturesque trolley.

Most Belgian cities have these trams, which was a bit of a problem because Dave and I aren't familiar with the road etiquette of accommodating them. So we took the subconscious decision to ignore them, a strategy that seemed to stand us in good stead until we arrived in Ghent. Ghent is a very ancient, small city with a one-way system that would addle even the sharpest of navigators. Some streets are one way for all traffic, others for cars and bikes, for lorries or for pedestrians and cyclists, but the trams seemed to go where the hell they liked. Faced with one coming towards you at some speed, ignoring the ruddy thing is no longer an option. So be warned, pull over if you can or else close your eyes and hope for the best (though I must confess Dave and I have adopted this 'hope for the best' technique around the world with varying degrees of success).

DAVE: We had come to Ghent to sample waterzooi, a fish soup-cum-stew that is one of the classic dishes of the Belgian kitchen. For centuries, two great rivers, the Schelde and the Leie, have flowed through Ghent. Where the rivers meet, huge amounts of freshwater fish used to be caught and waterzooi made from them. Nowadays, the soup is usually made with fish from the North Sea (never a great fan of eating river fish, I bet this actually tastes better).

The fish is cooked in a steaming, creamy broth. Think of it like a bouillabaisse, but with cushions thrown in – it's a much comfier dish. You start with a good fish stock and some vegetables like carrots, celery and potatoes, some bay leaves, thyme and cream. The fish, prawns and perhaps mussels are then added to steam. It's a pure dish and really lovely.

FINCH WARBLING

SI: The trip from Ghent to the tiny village of Hulste, home of the Finch Warble Counting Championship museum, takes you halfway across Belgium. In other words, it's another rain-lashed half an hour or so. But this was our first foray into the countryside and our first real taste of the frontier madness that seems to be part of every Belgian's heritage. In this pretty agricultural village more than sixty people turned up, reeking of fine beer at eleven on a cold, wet Sunday morning (is there some sort of theme developing here?). All were armed with their decorated finch cages, tiny stools and bits of chalk. They then settled down in the rain along a roadside ditch to make little marks on the competition sticks every time a warble came out of the cage in front of them.

Had we gone mad? What were we doing out here, surrounded by these solemn loonies all scraping away at their sticks? We walked up and down the line, giving each competitor the thumbs up (best not to provoke them, right?). Gradually the sheer intensity of their concentration sucked us in. Not such an odd sport after all, perhaps.

> 'Had we gone mad? What were we doing out here, surrounded by these solemn loonies all scraping away at their sticks? We walked up and down the line, giving each competitor the thumbs up (best not to provoke them, right?).' SI

DAVE: This sport has been around a long time and I really fancied having a go. My Dad used to breed budgies so I reckon it's in my blood to breed a super-chaffinch, a kind of Pavarotti of the bird world. Ooh, let that rip on a Sunday morning: England 1, Belgium nil pwoints.

SI: But at the end of the hour, when the final whistle blew, the joke was on us. None of the finchateers had finches in their cages – just MP3 players playing recordings of finches long gone south for the winter. Those plucky little Belgians were having a laugh.

BRUSSELS AND BOWLER HATS

DAVE: Yes, strange sense of humour these folk have. And it comes to a peak in Brussels, home of the European Parliament and the cartoon capital of the world. Belgians love cartoons. The country was the birthplace of Hergé, who created the world-famous character of Tintin in 1929. Since then, the books have been translated into dozens of languages all over the world, turning Tintin, his loyal dog Snowy, Professor Calculus, Captain Haddock and the Thompson Twins into legends. All over Brussels there are murals and statues taken straight from comic books. There is even a cartoon museum where we found ourselves gaining a deeper understanding of Belgium's unique contribution to the world, including the one export we just can't forgive the country for: the Smurfs. A tribe of little blue fellows with only one girl (a smurfette) is surely the result of a bad acid trip? Anyone for smurfing?

We also had a total epiphany at the museum. Standing in front of a mural of Thompson and Thompson, the intrepid Tintin detectives, falling about in their bowler hats and black suits and clutching their canes, we suddenly declared: 'They look just like the bowler-hatted man who keeps appearing in Magritte's paintings!'

So we rushed to the Magritte museum, and it was true. René Magritte's house is quite ordinary and the juxtaposition between this and his extraordinary work is striking. Magritte was born in 1898 and in his day his work was considered revolutionary, political and dangerous. The surrealists deliberately set out to undermine bourgeois convention, and famous images, like the man in a bowler hat with a green apple covering his face, are haunting and provocative.

This image also led us to thinking about Brussels' European Parliament and its bowler-hatted bureaucrats. We were definitely on to something. Most of us have heard rumours about EC food regulations and policies. You know the sort of thing: straight bananas, tomatoes with no dimples and no more unpasteurized cheese. We decided to visit the European Parliament to find out more. It was shut.

SI: It turned out that the parliament was sitting that week in Strasbourg. Well, Strasbourg's not even in Belgium, but we were going to hunt these people down even if it meant driving over to . . . oh yes, France. After all, it wouldn't be much of a detour, would it? Nothing's more than half an hour away from anywhere in Belgium. Were we wrong! We set off in the rain (no surprises there) and quicker than a herd of turtles. Yes, five and a half hours later, we found ourselves in Strasbourg, another beautiful medieval city, but in the wrong country.

DAVE: We took some time out before we met the great and the good, to drive up into the vineyard-crowded hills above the city. There we feasted on sweet Alsace wine from those very vineyards and crunchy baguettes with duck foie gras and baked our own version of the classic quiche Lorraine. Now don't laugh. Real blokes do eat quiche and a real quiche Lorraine isn't one of those custard pies filled with anything from salmon and broccoli to chicken and West Highland terrier. Real quiche is a butch, simple tart made from eggs, smoky bacon, crème fraîche and Gruyère (see our recipe). Anyway, back to the suits.

SI: The MEPs we talked to were surprisingly frank. When asked why it seemed that most EU legislation favoured large-scale food manufacturers rather than small to medium artisanal producers, it seemed that money was the core issue. This is because the more money you have, the more political contacts you can lobby and dine and the better the chances of getting legislation through that favours you.

DAVE: After hearing from the MEPs about the EC's strict hygiene regulations and controversial laws such as the fishing policy, it seemed to us that interesting foods will continue to be available, but at a price. The rich will still be able to indulge, but the rest of us will be prevented from getting access to the good stuff. Farmers' markets are great, but they tend to be expensive. Why should good, un-buggered-about-with food be the preserve of the select few? It should be the norm. It always used to be when every town had a market.

SI: Now don't switch off, because the politics of food is important and, whether you realize it or not, we as customers have the power. It's about supply and demand. If we buy bad food, then there will always be a food processing company there to manufacture it. Convenience food isn't cheap, but with the pressures of time, children, work and life in general, it is becoming more and more difficult to source, prepare, cook and eat the food we want. This is why all us workaday folk should take a more active role in the celebration of the food culture of the UK. At the moment it can cost a lot of money to participate, but good food should be financially accessible to everyone. We seem to have forgotten the roots of our food, but all we need to do is remember what our mothers and grandmothers made in the kitchen. It really is that simple.

HUNTING HAIRY BOARS

DAVE: Being a land with a massive amount of forest in the shape of the Ardennes, it's no coincidence that in Belgium, hunting and eating game are very popular. We were lucky to be introduced to Madame Verbeke, who has hunted all over the world. She was a charming lady with many wonderful stories to tell, her walls decked with hunting trophies. She seemed to take a bit of a fancy to our cameraman and we wondered if there was a chance he would end up there, stuffed in between a wildebeest and a boar. I think as a stuffed, grizzly Scot he would have looked OK.

Deep in the fabled forests of the Ardennes, where wild boar have run free since time immemorial and been chased by Belgian hunters since lunchtime, we tiptoed around with Madame Verbeke's gamekeeper, looking for quarry. At least, we were pretending to for the cameras because no self-respecting boar would be around at this time of year. But suddenly, unbelievably, a huge one broke cover just about a hundred feet from us and went crashing through the undergrowth. It looked like a hairy biker, but bigger, and hungrier. How we laughed when we realized our cameraman missed the shot completely!

Madame Verbeke took us to visit her butcher instead, where the game on sale is brought in by hunters. The meat is butchered and packed there and then sold from the shop next door. With all our concerns about food miles (the distance food has to travel from the producer to the consumer and the time and fuel used to get it there), this was a model operation. Madame Verbeke bought two whole wild boar loins, which were expertly cooked back at her house in a sauce of myrtle berries and green peppercorns and eaten with a potato and celeriac mash. It was heaven.

'All was going swimmingly, when suddenly we were set upon by the cowboys, chased down the field and roped up. We didn't quite know what had hit us. Maybe these hard honchos had heard we'd cooked quiche a couple of days earlier.' SI

Madame Verbeke's wild boar is wonderful and makes the most free-range bacon you could ever come across. We are both great fans of eating game because it tends to be really healthy. It runs wild, so is completely free-range, it is low in fat and cholesterol and is killed humanely.

SI: The Ardennes is also home to yet another example of bonkers Belgium: the Dave City dude ranch. Who would have thought that there's some corner of a foreign field (well, in southern Belgium) where the Wild West rules supreme. Every Saturday, up to fifty horsemen from all over the area put on leather chaps and sashay down to Dave City to ride around the corral, twirl lassos and sneak up on unsuspecting local cattle, hot brands in hand.

Thanks to Madame Verbeke's butcher, we had a bunch of wild boar meat to use up, so we set down in the mud to cook two more Belgian national dishes, flamande and stoemp, for those hungry cowboys. Flamande is usually made with beef cooked in a couple of gallons of dark beer, but it's even better with local boar, and for the stoemp we planned to add Brussels sprouts to the mashed potatoes. All was going swimmingly (that weather thing again), when suddenly we were set upon by the cowboys, chased down the field and roped up. We didn't quite know what had hit us. Maybe these hard honchos had heard we'd cooked quiche a couple of days earlier, or perhaps, in these parts, they just don't like Brussels sprouts.

THE FOOD

DAVE: Belgium, land of chips and horse steak? Well, yes, but it is also home to some of the greatest food you can eat, from everyday 'peasant' food to the best haute cuisine in the world. It has what I call a real yum factor. You know, that sort of 'lick your lips, you know you want to' kind of thing. I think Belgium might be Europe's best-kept food secret.

THE PERFECT CHIP

The foundation of all Belgian food has to be the chip. You can be as snotty as you like, but 99 per cent of all humans love a good chip and the Belgians are no different. They just love potatoes. It is said that the best chips in Belgium are to be found in the little green huts on the square in Bruges. They sell a lot of chips, but they do have to because their rent is 100,000 Euros per year (and potatoes don't grow on trees, you know).

The Belgian chip shop doesn't serve fish, but you do get a selection of dips. The most common is home-made mayonnaise (see our great bulletproof recipe for this). Alternatively, you can get beery gravy or Ardennes sauce, which is nice and spicy. Order a portion of **bitterballen**, little tangy Dutch meatballs that make you crave beer, try cheese croquettes or some of the plentiful sausages. God, this stuff is good. Not every day, mind, or it's down to coronary care for you, Sonny Jim.

The perfect partner to your perfect chips is a bowl of mussels. The Belgian coast is a seafood lover's paradise and the moules are great here, cooked like regular moules marinière, but with the addition of thyme, cream and often a bit of celery. It is a constant mystery to me why we British folk don't love our seafood more. The coast of Belgium is only around 60 kilometres long, whilst we have thousands of miles of coast and we can't cut it. What's wrong with us?

BELGIAN CHOCOLATE

The other obvious Belgian biggy is chocolate, or Chocolat (ooh, Juliette Binoche, she can be my fondant fancy any day of the week). Belgian chocolate is sensuous, delicious and the way they present it in Belgium is as an art form. We went to the lovely medieval city of Namur to see one of the greatest chocolatiers in the country, Monsieur Galler. The first thing that struck us was that he bore a great resemblance to Willy Wonka. I did mention this and he laughed. I don't think it was the first time someone had noticed.

Belgium used to have a lot of African colonies, including the Congo, and the cocoa beans produced there are stronger and have a fuller flavour than South American beans. Combine these beans with the skills of a fine French pâtissier and you get some idea of what Monsieur Galler's chocolates are like. And even the smallest box will be exquisitely packaged, fancier than Marie Antoinette's garters.

Praline is the top Belgian choc, a glassily sculpted dark shell with a soft centre that can be a silken ganache, fluffy crème fraîche or a regular nutty praline. A lot of these are 85 per cent cocoa solids and very light on the sugar, so have a sophisticated, adult taste.

The chocolatiers are celebrities. Everybody has their favourite and ours has to be Monsieur Galler. Not only does he make amazing pralines, he produces tasting kits that mix together strange but exciting flavours like cardamoms and strawberries with balsamic vinegar. He also has boxes of chocolates called Les Florales made from flower petals. Some are the usual rose or violet creams, but others are flavoured with tastes like jasmine and orange. They are exquisite.

Monsieur Galler even has a restaurant attached to his shop, producing gastronomic food, but with chocolate at its heart. This is no gimmick. The food is sublime. We feasted there on lobster tails in a white chocolate sauce, followed by fillet of hare in a dark chocolate sauce. Remember, until you put sugar in chocolate, it is a savoury creature. After all this talk, do try our chocolate mousse recipe. We managed to extract it from our Belgian location manager's granny. It's a heavy one, but the real deal.

THE BEER

DAVE: Beer is the national drink of Belgium – and of bikers. The country is hop heaven, with more than six hundred different brews available at any one time. There is almost no wine produced because of the climate, but that climate is great for growing grains and Belgian brewers make beer with the same application and care that a French winemaker devotes to producing fine wines.

In Belgium you find a vast and mysterious world of spicy, fruity, hoppy, sweet and sour ales, from the palest brews to beers as black as Guinness. The strength varies from a modest 4 per cent to a mind-blowing 12 per cent. Wine can clock in at around 12 per cent, so four pints of this strong beer? I don't think so . . . well, not very often!

'Beer is the national drink of Belgium – and of bikers.' DAVE

The story of beer goes back to the Middle Ages. The average person in those days drank loads of beer, not just to get bladdered, but because the water was so bad and polluted. What a great excuse when you come home from the pub, 'I'm sorry I'm in a state, love, the water was bad again.'

In Belgium, brewers sprung up in every city, producing beer unique to the place. The brewers were dependent on local ingredients and used a mixture of herbs called gruit to give aroma, taste and a bitterness to what was basically a sweet mash. As with most great inventions, there was a turning point – an epiphany. Towards the end of the fourteenth century the Dutch arrived in Belgium, bringing with them a love of orange T-shirts, rubbery cheese, bland tomatoes and beer made with hops. The Belgian brewers seized the latter with relish because Belgian gruitbeer tasted like goat's piss compared with the fine hoppy Dutch ales. Before long, herbs were out and hops were in (though Belgium has never produced a lot of its own hops, relying instead on imports, including our very own Kent hops).

TRAPPIST BEERS

DAVE: Trappist beers are the very best beers there are. The Church once owned much of Belgium's most fertile land and so grew the finest crops, producing the greatest beer. Trappist beers range from gold to dark in colour, are very distinctive in taste and have a great ability to make your feet melt. The Dubbel is dark and about twice the strength of a simple brew. The Tripel is golden and, at three times the strength, weighs in at around 10 per cent.

The Trappist monks are members of the strict Cistercian order and today there are just six Trappist monasteries still brewing, namely Westmalle, Westvleteren, Achel, Chimay, Orval and Rochefort.

Westmalle produces the strong golden Westmalle Tripel, which must rank as one of the best beers in the world. Please seek this one out. Like pilgrims to a holy shrine, we made our way to the brewery north of Antwerp. We expected to be met by rosy-cheeked, porky Friar Tucks who would clasp us to their beery bosoms. Not a bit of it. We couldn't get anywhere near. The brewery was like a secure military compound. All we saw were lorry loads of liquid gold furtively leaving the premises.

Orval make one beer only and it's spectacular. Wonderfully golden and complex, this hoppy and very bitter beer is great to cook with and we used it when we cooked the wild boar flamande for the Dave City cowboys.

The brewery we filmed at was Rochefort. This place is a little piece of heaven and if you are in any doubt, sink a couple of their 11.3 per cent beers to put you on a cloud. The brewing monks' long day starts at 3:30 a.m. (imagine that with a hangover) and continues until 5:00 p.m. They produce three beers. The number six is brewed mostly for local consumption, while the ten is a very chocolaty, caramel-dark beer, great for sipping in front of a roaring log fire.

WHEAT BEERS

Next, we have the white, or wheat, beers. Quite simply, they are very refreshing, cloudy, pale beers made from wheat. The most popular is Hoegaarden, which we get in the UK. This is particularly nice with a slice of lemon on a hot summer day. Hoegaarden was first brewed for the old folk in the 1960s, but it wasn't long before the trendies took over and it became a global brand. In Belgium, the beer connoisseur's top brews are the white beers of Louvain.

The Champagne of wheat beers is Lambic, which, befittingly for a capital city, is the beer of Brussels. The beer contains a wild yeast that gives the drink its natural sparkle. Lambics take up to three years to brew and can be an acquired taste because they tend to be quite sharp and fruity. The most popular is Gueuze, a blend of different Lambics that reminds me of cider. It's delicious with roast pork.

'Next, we have the white, or wheat, beers. Quite simply, they are very refreshing, cloudy, pale beers made from wheat.' DAVE

AND YET MORE BEERS

Now, to the fruit beers. These aren't all the sweet, sugary creatures that one might presume, although some are. The most famous is a dry cherry beer called Kriek and our recipe for cherry and almond cake with Kriek is a winner. There are also a number of raspberry, apricot and banana beers available.

Another category is the golden ales. These are a modern invention and have crept on to the Belgian beer bandwagon. The original of these is Duval, which translates literally as 'a taste that comes from the devil'. Duval was invented as a dark victory beer after World War One and it certainly got rid of trench foot and caused a few giggles. It was reinvented as a golden beer after World War Two, but appeared in its present incarnation in the 1970s along with Adam Ant and stack-heeled boots.

BEER GLASSES

Every Belgian beer must be drunk from a glass that has been invented for it, ensuring that the head is perfect to the very last drop. Many beer bottles even advise which glass you should use on their back label. Glasses from Trappist breweries tend to be shaped like a chalice or Holy Grail – the ones for Westmalle Tripel and Orval look like something from Raiders of the Lost Ark.

My favourite glass is for a beer called Kwak (yes, that's right, the noise a dyslexic duck makes). The glass is like a mini yard of ale and has a round bottom that makes it impossible to put it down on a table. In bars nowadays, they give you a wooden stand, but in the olden days, this glass wasn't a gimmick. It was called a coachman's glass, because whenever a coach stopped for a break, the coachman would sprint into the pub, grab a beer and run back out, resting his beer in a stand built into the coach. Of course, the coachman could get proper squiffy on his journey, but woe betide him if anyone nicked his horses while he was having a pint.

BLUE CHEESE STRAWS   MAKES 5-10

This is a super simple nibble that is great with a beer or, indeed, our royal gin fizz. You can adapt this how you like (try Parmesan or Cheddar cheese with sunflower seeds, for example) but the blue cheese and poppy seeds work well.

1 (500g) packet of puff pastry
200 g blue cheese (Gorgonzola, Dolcelatte or similar, even Danish Blue), crumbled
1 egg, beaten
1 heaped tablespoon poppy seeds

Preheat the oven to 180°C.

Roll out the pastry till very thin. Cover one half with the cheese, fold over the other half to sandwich the cheese, then roll it out (any escaped bits of cheese will eventually become nice chewy bits, so don't worry).

Keep rolling, folding the pastry over about three times. Cut into long strips (approximately 50cm long for big hairy fellers or 15cm for daintier types) and then twist like barley sugar.

Place the strips on a greased baking tray. Brush with the egg and scatter with the poppy seeds. Bake for 15 to 20 minutes on a high shelf in the oven till golden. 'Ooh I say, fancy another cheese straw, vicar?'

CHEESE CROQUETTES

MAKES 12 CROQUETTES AND SERVES 6

These are very similar to shrimp croquettes and sometimes
at Belgian restaurants you can have one shrimp and one
cheese instead of the normal serving of two of the same. The
mixture has to sit in the fridge overnight, so give yourself plenty
of time. They are great for vegetarians and are fantastic with a
nice big glass of red wine . . . 'Might one suggest a Pomerol, sir?'

for the croquettes

75g unsalted butter

100g plain flour

350ml milk

100g Parmesan cheese, grated

100g Emmental, grated

100g Gruyère, grated

3 egg yolks

½ teaspoon white pepper

¼ teaspoon freshly grated nutmeg

a pinch of cayenne pepper

for the coating

3 egg whites

100g plain flour

100g dried white breadcrumbs

vegetable oil, for deep-frying

lettuce leaves, to serve

deep-fried curly parsley, to serve

Melt the butter in a saucepan over a medium heat, add the flour and mix like Fatboy Slim in the zone for a couple of minutes, keeping the mixture moving around the base of the pan. Whisk in the milk slowly and carry on whisking for 3 minutes until smooth and thick. Add the cheeses and stir continuously until it has become a great, heavy cheese sauce.

Remove the sauce from the heat and allow to cool slightly. Stir in the egg yolks, one at a time, and then add the white pepper, nutmeg and cayenne pepper. Taste before adding some salt because, as we have observed before, cheese can be a salty beast.

Line a 23cm square cake tin with clingfilm and pour in the mixture, spreading it evenly. Refrigerate overnight to set.

Next day, cut out sausage-sized rectangles of the mixture and roll into cylinders. Lightly beat the egg whites until frothy in one bowl. Put the flour in another bowl and the breadcrumbs in another.

Heat the oil in a pan or deep-fat fryer to around 200°C.

Dip the cylinders into the flour, then dip into the egg whites. Shake off the excess. Dredge in the breadcrumbs and deep-fry in batches for about 2 to 3 minutes till golden brown and crisp. Keep the croquettes warm in the oven while you do the rest.

Serve the croquettes on a bed of lettuce leaves with a heap of deep-fried curly parsley. (To deep-fry the parsley, plunge it into the oil for 1–2 minutes, remove and drain on a piece of kitchen paper to absorb the excess oil. It will be dark green, crispy and sort of delicious – it's a Belgian thing!)

BANGING BELGIAN ONION SOUP

SERVES 10 AS A STARTER OR 6 AS A HEARTY LUNCH

Forget ya fancy French onion soup, let this stick to ya ribs.

75g butter

1kg onions, sliced

2 large leeks, well washed
and sliced

2 large potatoes,
peeled and chopped

330ml bottle of Belgian beer
(such as Leffe)

1 litre chicken stock
(or vegetable stock if
you want to keep the
dish vegetarian)

3 bay leaves

a sprig of thyme

salt and white pepper

200g Gruyère cheese, grated

2 heaped tablespoons
chopped chives

a pinch or grating of fresh nutmeg

In a very large pan with a lid, melt the butter, add the onion and leek and cook over a medium heat until translucent – about 10 to 15 minutes should do it. Stir regularly as you don't want the onion or leek to brown (never forget, a brown onion is an unhappy onion, especially in a white soup).

Stir in the potato. Add the lager, bring to the boil and cook for a couple of minutes until there is a little less liquid.

Add the stock, bay leaves, thyme and some seasoning, bring back up to the boil, turn the heat down and simmer for 25 minutes with the lid on until all the veggies are cooked through. Remove the thyme and bay leaves.

Blitz half the quantity of soup in a blender until smooth, then return the blended soup to the lumpy broth and stir together – this gives lots of lovely texture.

To serve, spoon the soup into bowls and add a handful of the cheese to each bowl. Finish with a good sprinkling of chives and nutmeg.

For an additional twist, you could add a crouton topped with more cheese and a chive flower (only do the last bit if it's your boss coming for dinner and you're asking for more money).

BEER AND CHEESE BREAD   SERVES 6

We love bread recipes. We found this bread at one of the many Trappist monasteries that produce good bread and beer – the source of life and good enough to give a monk bad habits!!! Great with our onion soup.

250ml strong beer (such as Chimay)
4 teaspoons sugar
1 tablespoon (30g) dried yeast
600g strong white bread flour
320g wholemeal flour
200g Cheddar cheese, grated
75g Parmesan cheese, grated

50g powdered milk
1½ teaspoons salt
1½ teaspoons mustard powder
2 eggs, beaten
2 teaspoons fennel seeds
1 egg white

Pour the beer into a saucepan and warm it gently until it is blood temperature. Then, in a large bowl, dissolve the sugar and yeast in the warm beer and let stand for 5 minutes.

Keep 80g of the white flour aside and place the rest in a separate bowl with the wholemeal flour. Add the cheeses, milk powder, salt, mustard, eggs and fennel seeds. Stir in the yeast mixture and keep mixing until you have a soft dough. Turn the dough out on to a floured surface and knead for about 20 minutes until smooth and elastic. Add the remaining flour as needed to prevent the dough sticking. Should the dough become too dry, sprinkle warm water on to it as you knead.

Place the dough on a large baking tray and brush with the egg white. Cover the bread with a tea towel and leave to rise in a warm, dry and draught-free place for 1 to 2 hours until the dough doubles in size. Preheat the oven to 200°C. Slash or criss-cross the dough and bake for 20 minutes until gorgeous and crusty on the outside. To check the bread is cooked, turn it upside-down using a tea towel and tap its bottom. If it sounds hollow, it's ready, but if not, pop it back in the oven for another 5 minutes.

BELGIAN FRITES, OR THE BEST CHIPS YOU HAVE EVER TASTED

The Belgians are bazonkers about chips. None of this chunky chip or skinny chip nonsense, just perfect chips, soft in the middle and crispy on the outside. It's hard to believe it, but they eat even more chips than a Geordie lass coming home from the pub.

potatoes (good old potatoes like
  King Edwards, Maris Pipers,
  Desirée, or Cyprus if you're
  feeling flush)

clean vegetable oil

sea salt

chip-shop malt vinegar

Cut as many chips as you like, not too thick and not too thin.

Wash under cold water to get rid of the starch and, if you have the time, it's worth letting the cut chips soak in cold water overnight. Blot dry on some kitchen roll.

The secret of good chips is to cook them twice. You need a deep-fat fryer or a chip pan with a thermometer so you can heat the oil to 130°C.

Cook the chips in batches for about 10 minutes. They will not brown, but will cook through to the middle. Set aside on kitchen paper and leave to cool (they can be left for several hours).

Heat the oil up to 190°C and cook the chips for about 5 minutes till crispy and golden.

Ooh, we love chips . . . who doesn't? Go on, spoil yourself. Serve with sea salt flakes and malt vinegar.

FOOLPROOF MAYONNAISE

You can't have chips in Belgium without a good mayonnaise to go with them. For this bombproof version we use a food processor, although you could just as easily use a whisk or fork.

2 egg yolks

1 whole egg

1 tablespoon Dijon mustard

juice of ½ lemon

½ teaspoon salt

½ teaspoon ground black pepper

½ teaspoon caster sugar

400ml vegetable oil

Place everything in the food processor except the oil. Blitz for 10 seconds to combine, then pour in the oil in a very slow but steady stream. When the oil is all in, blitz for another 10 seconds and there you have it, perfect mayonnaise. You will never buy a jar again.

Play around with your mayonnaise, adding lemon or lime zest for a citrus mayo or garlic to make a garlic mayo as strong or as subtle as you like.

MUSSELS   SERVES 4

This is almost the national dish of Belgium and by 'eck they do it well. Served with their perfect chips, it is a union made in heaven, a Fred and Ginger, a Homer and Marge of the food world . . . It simply works. The Belgians do their mussels in a slightly different way from the French and I think their version has more taste. So flex your muscles and have a go.

2kg mussels

50g unsalted butter

3 large shallots, chopped

2 sticks of celery, chopped

1 leek, finely chopped

2 bay leaves

2 tablespoons finely
  chopped fresh parsley

1 sprig of fresh thyme

1 teaspoon ground black pepper

300ml dry white wine
  (use good stuff)

200ml double cream

Firstly, clean the mussels. Scrub them and then take away their beards (that's the tiny Brillo-pad bit near the hinge). They should be alive (give them a tap: if they close, they are alive, but if not, throw them out). Wash under cold running water and cook soon after cleaning.

Melt the butter in a big pan and add the shallot, celery, leek and bay leaves. Cook over a medium heat until softened but not brown.

Add the mussels, half the parsley, the thyme and sprinkle on the pepper. Pour in the wine, bring to the boil, cover and steam for around 3 minutes. They are ready when they have all opened (throw away any that don't open as they will be bad). Pour in the cream.

Serve in big bowls, garnished with the remaining parsley.

FISHCAKES WITH PARSLEY SAUCE
AND BABY LEEKS   SERVES 4

This is another step up the croquette and Belgian rissole ladder. There is such great seafood on the North Sea coast, which can be used in our recipe for a yummy traditional favourite. You can't beat a well-made parsley sauce and the bed of baby leeks gives you an ace complete meal.

500ml vegetable stock

2 bay leaves

200g white fish fillets
  (we love haddock)

12 baby leeks

1 dressed crab
  (don't forget the brown meat!)

1 tablespoon capers,
  washed and drained

zest of ½ lemon

2 tablespoons chopped chives

salt and white pepper

500g cold mashed potato
  (this is a great way to
  use up last night's mash)

2 eggs, separated

2 good handfuls of
  home-made breadcrumbs

vegetable oil, for shallow frying
  (enough to cover bottom
  of your pan with ½cm)

125ml double cream

2 tablespoons fresh parsley,
  chopped

25g plain flour

25g butter

Add the stock and bay leaves to a shallow pan, bring to the boil and then add the fish and leeks. Reduce the heat to a slow simmer and poach the fish and leeks for around 7 minutes until the fish is cooked and the leeks are tender.

Remove the fish and flake the flesh, taking care to get rid of any skin and bones. Set aside the leeks for later and continue to simmer the stock until the liquid has reduced by half.

To the fish add the crab, capers, lemon zest, chives and some seasoning. When blended, fold in the potato and egg yolk. Form four lovely big fishcakes or eight little fancy-pants ones.

Lightly beat the egg white in one bowl. Put the breadcrumbs in another. Dip the fishcakes in the egg white and coat in crumbs.

Heat the oil in a shallow frying pan to a gentle rumble (too hot and the fishcakes will burn and not cook inside, too cold and they will become

a soggy mess). Cook till golden (it's difficult to give a cooking time because it depends on the thickness of your fishcakes),

While the fishcakes are cooking, make your parsley sauce. Heat up the reduced stock and add the cream. Bring to a rolling boil (where the water is bubbling so hard you can't stir it down). Add the parsley, then whisk in the **beurre manié** (the **beurre manié** is the flour and butter blended together and we use it to thicken the sauce in this and a lot of our other recipes). When thick, the sauce is ready and will have all the taste from the poached fish and leeks and a great silky texture from the **beurre manié**.

Place the leeks on a really hot griddle pan and sear till chargrilled. At the last minute, add a knob of butter. This will sizzle up and give the leeks a nutty flavour.

Lay the leeks on the plates, top with the fishcakes, then pour over the sauce. These are seriously good fishcakes.

WATERZOOI SERVES 4

Fish waterzooi is particular to Ghent in Belgium. We ate it in a really small backstreet restaurant and it was, without doubt, one of the best dishes we have tried on our travels. Use the best fish available or whatever you want to eat, because it really doesn't matter what kind of fish you choose.

50g butter

2 shallots, finely chopped

1 leek, white part only, julienned (cut into fine sticks thinner than matchsticks)

2 carrots, peeled and julienned

½ small celeriac, peeled and julienned

1 stick of celery, julienned

1 large potato, peeled and diced

2 bay leaves

a good sprig of thyme

a pinch of saffron

½ litre fish stock

a small glass of white wine

3 egg yolks

200ml double cream

salt and pepper

chopped fresh parsley

the fish we used

250g salmon fillets, skinned

250g bream fillets, skinned

250g sea bass fillets, skinned

250g haddock fillets, skinned

250g raw shell-on prawns

In a large but deep frying pan, melt the butter and cook the shallot without colouring over a medium heat until soft. Add all the remaining vegetables, the bay leaves, the thyme, the saffron, the stock and white wine, cover with a lid and simmer gently for 10 to 15 minutes until the potato is tender.

Uncover and add the salmon, bream, bass and haddock in a single layer on top of the vegetables and cook for 10 minutes.

Remove the fish and the vegetables from the stock with a slotted spoon and set aside on a warm plate. Remove the thyme and bay leaves and discard.

Mix the egg yolks and double cream together, add a ladleful of hot, but not boiling, stock and mix well. Pour this mixture back into the stock in the frying pan and heat for a couple of minutes, stirring continuously. DO NOT ALLOW TO BOIL OR THE MIXTURE WILL CURDLE! Season with salt and pepper.

Divide the vegetables into four large soup bowls, then place the fish on top. Ladle over the sauce, add a handful of prawns, sprinkle with parsley and serve. Get your laughing gear around this!

QUICHE LORRAINE SERVES 6

This is a truly simple but perfect quiche. It originates from the Alsace area and everyone we spoke to about the recipe had the same ingredients, so we know it's true and accurate. It also goes to prove that real men eat quiche – well, so Dave says, the big poof!

for the pastry
180g plain flour
100g cold unsalted butter
50g Parmesan cheese, grated
2 teaspoons chopped fresh thyme
1 egg yolk

for the filling
3 eggs
150g pancetta, chopped
250ml crème fraîche
150g Gruyère, grated
ground black pepper to taste

Preheat the oven to 180°C.

To make the pastry, keep your hands and kitchen cool. Sieve the flour into a mixing bowl. Dice the cold butter and add it to the flour with the Parmesan and thyme. Using the tips of your fingers, rub the butter into the cheesy, herby, floury mixture until it forms crumblike pieces. Add the egg yolk and water and keep mixing until it forms a dough. A little more water might be necessary. Wrap the dough in clingfilm and put it into the fridge for at least 30 minutes.

On a floured surface, roll out your pastry to fit one large tart tin. Carefully line the tin with the pastry, making sure that there are no holes in the bottom. Place a circle of baking paper over the pastry and fill with beans or rice or baking beans if you have them. Place the tin in the oven for 15 minutes. Then remove the beans and the baking paper before returning the tin to the oven for a further 5 minutes.

For the filling, add all the ingredients other than 50g of the Gruyère to a mixing bowl and stir gently to avoid filling the mixture with air.

Spoon your filling into your tart tin and sprinkle the remaining Gruyère over the top.

Cook for 15 minutes or until the filling is set – it should have a firm wobble. Allow to cool and serve with a mountain of green salad.

FLEMISH CHICKEN WITH
PRUNES AND BEER   SERVES 4

This great recipe is traditionally made with rabbit, so you can replace one chicken with two rabbits if you fancy bringing out the Fleming in yourself. A sweet and savoury vibe with a beer twist – it's a belter.

1 teaspoon salt

½ teaspoon ground black pepper

5 tablespoons plain flour

1 chicken, jointed (get your butcher to do this for you or buy chicken portions)

3 tablespoons vegetable oil

50g unsalted butter

150g lardons or 4 rashers of streaky bacon, chopped

2 onions, 1 sliced and 1 chopped

2 large carrots, chopped

2 tablespoons cider vinegar

4 cloves of garlic

2 bay leaves

4 cloves

2 sprigs of thyme

10 juniper berries

1 cinnamon stick

2 x 330ml bottles of wheat beer (we use Hoegaarden)

12 presoaked prunes, stoned (always like stoned prunes!)

100g raisins

Mix the salt, pepper and flour together in a bowl. Add the chicken pieces and mix well so they are covered with the flour.

Heat the oil and half the butter in a large sauté or frying pan with a lid. Sauté the chicken pieces in batches over a medium heat until golden brown (if you put them all in at once, they'll steam, which is a bad thing). Set aside the chicken once browned.

Add the lardons or bacon rashers to the pan and quickly fry them, then remove when golden brown. Add the two onions and carrot to the same pan and brown slightly.

Place the chicken and lardons back into the pan with the carrot and onions, add the vinegar and let the sauce cook, reducing slightly to take away the sharpness. Add the garlic, bay leaves, cloves, thyme, juniper berries and cinnamon.

Pour in the beer and add the remaining butter, cover with the lid and bring to the boil. Reduce the heat and gently simmer for 1 hour. Add the prunes and raisins and simmer for a further 20 minutes or until the fruit starts to break down. We suggest serving the chicken with buttered boiled potatoes and a parsley flourish!

ARDENNES PORK CHOPS WITH CIDER AND CARAMELIZED APPLES   SERVES 2

The Ardennes, land of the wild boar and pig, is situated on Belgium's border with France and the cooking is more French in style. This wonderful dish of pork chops (or wild boar) with a creamy cider sauce and caramelized apples is a reflection of the musky autumn days in the area's dense woodlands.

The great surprise here is how tender and juicy the chops become when you griddle them first to seal in the flavour and then poach them in the sauce. Please, please keep to the timings and you won't go wrong. Go on, make a pig of yourself!

2 pork chops

2 teaspoons sea salt

1 onion, finely chopped

75g smoked bacon, chopped

1 bouquet garni (you can buy this mix in any large supermarket)

150g button mushrooms

150g shallots, peeled

250ml Normandy cider

2 apples, peeled, cored and quartered

2 teaspoons Dijon mustard

200ml fresh double cream

salt and pepper

Roll the fat of the pork chops in the salt flakes (this will help colour and crisp the fat). Preheat both a griddle pan and a large non-stick frying pan (don't be put off by the idea of cooking on two pans at the same time – honest, it's easy).

Stand the pork chops fat-side down on the hot griddle pan. You may have to hold them with tongs to keep them upright, or use your fingers if you're feeling lucky, punk!

In the frying pan, sauté the onion and bacon over a medium heat until slightly coloured (not a lot, just a little, missus).

Back to the griddle pan:

Brown the chops on both sides to give the pork nice stripy markings.

Back to the frying pan:

In the meantime, add the bouquet garni, button mushrooms and shallots and cook for 3 to 4 minutes. Pour in the cider and bring to the boil, then add the pork chops and any juices from the griddle pan and cook for 10 minutes. Do not wash the griddle pan, instead keep it on a low heat to cook the apples.

Back to the griddle pan:

Add the apples and cook for 5 to 10 minutes until the apples are caramelized and coloured but don't fall to bits.

Back to the frying pan:

Remove the pork chops from the pan and set aside to rest. Bring the sauce in the pan up to the boil, add the mustard and cream and season to taste. Cook the sauce for another 4 to 5 minutes until it is a little less liquid.

Pour the sauce over your caramelized apples and pork chops. We suggest serving with a carrot purée and boiled potatoes.

BLIND FINCHES IN BEER GRAVY   SERVES 4

Nothing to do with little birds with eyesight problems, but a lovely ancient Belgian dish that we cooked for the finch fanciers of Hulste. It makes a great family supper dish with proper Belgian chips (we all love gravy with our chips).

for the filling

250g minced pork

1 egg yolk

1 teaspoon dried sage

1 tablespoon finely chopped shallot

1 tablespoon finely chopped curly parsley

1 heaped teaspoon Dijon mustard

4 thin slices of sirloin steak (50-75g each)

4 thin slices of good cooked ham (or Parma ham is nice too)

75g butter

1 tablespoon vegetable oil

12 shallots, quartered

150ml good Belgian beer (we use Leffe)

salt and black pepper to taste

2 teaspoons plain flour

To make the filling, mix all the ingredients together and season.

Next, take each sirloin steak and beat the living daylights out of it between two sheets of clingfilm until it is thinner than a thin thing. Lay the beaten steaks out flat and lay the ham on top. Place a quarter of the filling on each one, and then fold the steak over, tucking the ends in to make little parcels. Tie the parcels up with butcher's string so they look ready for the postbox (this is to stop them unwrapping as they cook). These can be set aside for later.

Heat 25g of the butter with the oil until hot, but not smoking, in a large frying pan. Add the meat parcels and brown all over (if it's hot enough, it shouldn't stick). This will take about 10 minutes. Remove the meat, then add the shallots and cook for about 5 minutes over a high heat until they turn a lovely caramel colour. Return the meat to the pan, add the beer, season with salt and pepper and bring to the boil, then reduce to a gentle simmer, cover and cook for 7 minutes.

After 7 minutes, have a look, turn the meat over and cook for another 7 minutes. Remove the meat parcels on to a warm plate and set aside.

Blend the remaining butter and the flour with a fork, then gradually whisk this thickening mixture into the gravy, making sure you get all the nice tasty bits in the pan worked in. Add more beer if it is too thick. Pour gravy over the meat and serve with loads of chips. Yum, yum.

STEAK WITH BÉARNAISE SAUCE SERVES 4

First, a few top tips about buying steak so that you'll have the perfect steak every time. The first point is BUY GOOD MEAT. Secondly, THE DARKER THE COLOUR OF THE MEAT, THE BETTER. If it's a light colour, don't buy it, because it'll be meat that hasn't been aged properly and has been pumped full of chemicals. Lastly, BUY STEAK MARBLED WITH SOME FAT because that's where the flavour is.

for the Béarnaise sauce
5 tablespoons tarragon vinegar
1 shallot, finely chopped
3 good sprigs of tarragon
6 peppercorns
1 bay leaf
4 egg yolks
250g melted butter
a splash of lemon juice

for the steak
4 generous steaks of your choice
a good grinding of mixed pepper for each steak

To make the Béarnaise sauce, add the vinegar, shallot, stalks from the tarragon, peppercorns and bay leaf to a saucepan. Bring to the boil slowly and boil for 2 to 3 minutes until the liquid has reduced by half. Strain into a clean jug.

Put the egg yolks in a blender and mix, then pour in the hot vinegar and continue to blend. Now, SLOWLY add the melted butter. The texture should be smooth and silky. Check the seasoning at this point, add the lemon and blend for another 30 seconds. At the last minute, add the roughly chopped tarragon leaves and blend for a further 30 seconds.

To cook your steak, make sure your frying pan or griddle pan is really hot. Season the steak with mixed pepper BUT NO SALT! Place it on the griddle and remember the general rule that the more you turn the meat, the tougher it gets.

I like my steak raw with its nose running and Dave likes it cooked a bit more than that, but not much more. As a rough guideline, cook it for 2 to 3 minutes on each side for medium rare. And like all meat, once the steak is cooked, LEAVE IT TO REST before you serve it.

CARBONADE A LA FLAMANDE, A.K.A. BEEF AND BEER STEW SERVES 4

Beef cooked in beer is part of the identity of Belgian cooking and this stew is particularly popular in Flanders. It's great comfort food for a winter's night and you don't need to faff for hours to make it.

Wandering the streets in Belgium, it's never long before you bump into a street vendor selling chips. When we stopped to eat, we found out that you can have a thinner version of this stew all over them. Ooh heaven, it's Belgium's equivalent of chips and gravy and it's totally lush.

2 tablespoons well-seasoned plain flour

1kg shin of beef (or good stewing beef) in chunks

75g butter

2 tablespoons vegetable oil

500g onions, sliced

a sprig of thyme

3 bay leaves

2 x 330ml bottles of dark brown beer (such as Chimay)

250ml beef stock

2 heaped tablespoons redcurrant jelly

1 tablespoon cider vinegar

Preheat the oven to 180°C.

Put the seasoned flour into a bowl and add the beef. Toss the beef in the flour until it is well coated. In a large oven-friendly pan with a lid, brown the meat in batches in the butter and oil over a medium-high heat until just browned all over, keeping the meat on the move in the bottom of the pan. Remove and set aside.

In the same pan, brown the onion for a couple of minutes. Return all the beef to the pan and turn the heat down to medium.

Add the herbs, beer and stock and then – ooh, we love this bit – deglaze the pan, scraping up all those lovely sticky bits from the bottom so they melt like a flip-flop on hot sand into the stew. Stir in the redcurrant jelly and the vinegar.

Place the lid on the pan and cook in the oven for 2 hours or until the meat is tender and the gravy is lovely and gloopy.

STOEMP, PRONOUCED STUMP! SERVES 4

Similar to colcannon and bubble and squeak, **stoemp** is one of those Belgian dishes that have loads of variations. Ours uses Brussels sprouts (well, we are in Belgium) and leeks. You can make a nice one with spinach to have with fish or one with carrots to go with pork, but this version goes wonderfully well with our beef and beer stew. Just the thing on Bonfire Night.

1kg good spuds
  (such as Maris Piper or Desirée)
250g Brussels sprouts,
  peeled and trimmed

150g leeks, chopped into chunks
a big knob of butter
100g fatty smoked bacon
1 onion, chopped

Cook the potatoes in a pan of boiling water for 15 to 20 minutes or until tender. When cooked, mash and set aside.

Boil the Brussels sprouts in salted water for about 5 to 7 minutes till tender. Cut into quarters and set aside. Boil the leeks in salted water for about 2 minutes to blanch, drain, run under cold water and set aside.

Melt the butter in a big frying pan, add the bacon and brown over a medium heat for 2 minutes. Turn down the heat, add the onion and cook until transparent.

Add the sprouts and leeks and cook gently for a couple of minutes to let the flavours marry, then mix in the mash and heat through. Adjust the seasoning to taste.

This is one way to get the nippers to eat sprouts.

ROYAL GIN FIZZ   MAKES 4

Apart from being a nation of hopheads, the Belgian folk are quite a nation of gin junkies. They drink Geneva gin, which is a complex drink far removed from the sometimes eau de cologne-like British supermarket gins. Indeed, there is a restaurant in Antwerp that serves some 500 different Geneva gins and has a restaurant that specializes in dishes cooked with Geneva gin. Anyone for salmon carpaccio with a Geneva gin dressing?

We used Geneva gin for this fine royal gin fizz, but you can just as easily use English gin. It's a great bittersweet treat that makes your toes curl.

100ml Geneva gin (or London will do)
4 teaspoons caster sugar
1 egg white
juice of 1 lemon
ice
a bottle of Champagne (or cheap fizz)

Place the gin, sugar, egg white and lemon juice in a blender with a couple of handfuls of ice.

Blitz, then pour into four highball glasses (or glasses of your choice) and top with the Champagne. You know, this one might even deserve a cherry on the top.

ALSACE APPLE PIE   SERVES 6-8

This is a top tart, fabulous hot or cold. It has a great cinnamon pastry base filled with spiced apple and topped with a light custard. An Alsatian that is definitely no dog.

for the pastry
250g plain flour
a pinch of salt
50g sugar
¼ teaspoon ground cinnamon
125g chilled unsalted butter, chopped
1 egg yolk

for the filling
100ml sweet white wine (like a Gewürztraminer or Riesling)
2 cloves

½ teaspoon ground ginger
¼ teaspoon ground cinnamon
1 tablespoon caster sugar
5 eating apples, peeled, cored and cut into thick slices

for the custard
75g caster sugar
200ml double cream
2 eggs, beaten
¼ teaspoon good vanilla extract

icing sugar, to decorate

First make the pastry by sieving the flour and mixing in the salt, sugar and cinnamon. Rub in the chopped butter with your fingertips until the flour goes crumblike. Add the egg yolk, mix, then gradually pour in from 1 to 3 tablespoons ice-cold water until the pastry binds together. Roll out the pastry and line a 20cm loose-bottomed, non-stick, round tart tin. Place this in the refrigerator to chill for 1 hour.

Preheat the oven to 180°C. Meanwhile, make the apple filling. Warm the wine, cloves, ginger, cinnamon and sugar in a pan with a lid for 3 minutes to infuse the flavours. Add the apples and simmer, with the lid on, for 10 minutes. Discard the cloves, remove the apples to a bowl and set aside. Cook the remaining liquid until it reduces to a toffeelike consistency. Pour over the apples and gently mix to coat.

Line the chilled pastry case with greaseproof paper and pour in old beans or baking beads. Bake for about 15 minutes, then remove the greaseproof paper and the beans and return to the oven for a further 5 minutes.

Mix all the custard ingredients together.

Spread the apples evenly into the pastry case. Pour over the custard and bake at 180°C for 20 minutes until the custard is set. Serve with a sprinkling of icing sugar.

CHERRY AND ALMOND FRUIT CAKE

SERVES 8–10

Belgian fruit beers are readily available in this country and fruit cake made with beer is a Belgian tradition (as is putting a glug of Newcastle Brown in a Geordie fruit cake). Our recipe uses Kriek, a cherry beer, and the cake is like a super-tasty cherry Genoa. Try it with a good lump of Lancashire or Cheddar cheese and an apple for your lunch.

250g butter
150g dark brown sugar
150g wholemeal flour
150g plain flour
1 teaspoon baking powder
1 teaspoon ground ginger
1 teaspoon ground cinnamon
1 teaspoon vanilla extract
4 eggs
150ml Kriek (Belgian cherry beer)

100g chopped almonds
100g raisins
100g dried cherries
200g glacé cherries
 (with natural colour please,
 not something off the top of
 an Essex girl's piña colada!)

for the glaze
2 tablespoons apricot jam
2 tablespoons Kriek

Preheat the oven to 180°C.

Cream the butter and sugar together (use a food processor if you like, this is a stress-free cake). Sieve the flours, the baking powder and the spices together and blend into the butter mixture. Don't be put off if the mixture appears dry at this stage. Add the vanilla.

Beat the 4 eggs together with the beer and gradually add to the mix, beating in well. Add the almonds, raisins and dried cherries to the mixture with half the glacé cherries, some whole, some halved.

Line a 23cm cake tin with greaseproof paper and tip in your mixture. Decorate with the remaining glacé cherries. Do not let the mixture sit before placing in the oven because the beer is already reacting with the baking powder and will be losing rising power.

Bake on a low shelf in the oven for 1 hour 15 minutes. Leave to cool in the tin. Mix the jam with the 2 tablespoons of beer and heat for a couple of minutes until the liquid is slightly reduced. Paint this on top of the cake to give it a lovely glaze and bask in the glory.

CHOCOLATE MOUSSE FROM BRUGES

SERVES 4

In Belgium you can't ignore chocolate – well anyway, who would want to? Mme van Innes, a lovely lady in Bruges, gave us this unbeatable family recipe for a really dense and heavy chocolate mousse. It is more like a chocolate pot than a mousse – so rich, you can stand your spoon up in it.

400g good dark chocolate (no less than 70% cocoa solids)

4 eggs, separated (yolks in one bowl, whites in another)

2½ tablespoons caster sugar

2 teaspoons Drambuie (optional)

double cream (optional)

Melt the chocolate in a bain-marie (i.e. in a bowl above a saucepan of lightly simmering water, making sure that the bubbling water does not touch the bowl) or stick it in a microwave. Once melted, let it cool a little and then stir in the egg yolks one by one. Stir in the sugar.

Beat the egg whites until stiff and fold into the chocolate mixture. At the last minute, gently stir in the Drambuie (if you fancy it) with the delicacy of Michelangelo painting your ceiling.

Place the mousse in glasses or cups and chill for 4 to 5 hours. Top with cream for that Irish coffee lookalike vibe.

Ta very much, Mrs van Innes.

MOROCCO

WESTERN SAHARA

MOROCCO

ALGERIA

Marrakech

Tamaloute

Oukaimeden

El-Kelaâ M'Gouna

Er-Rachidia

Ouarzazate

Merzouga

N

SI: You know how it is with some countries. You wait all year for that special holiday, that longed-for trip to somewhere you've always wanted to see. But when you get there, the first thing that strikes you is not the differences, but the similarities.

The weather's pretty much the same. They've got a Starbucks. The food is either their idea of what a western holidaymaker wants to eat or it's shipped in frozen from Solihull via big crates. She's wearing that dress you bought from Topshop a year ago, he's drinking a can of Heineken and the music you hear everywhere is Top 40 Lite.

But Morocco isn't like that. It's a cultural swat to the side of the head, a big, booming bash to the senses. The light, the colours, the smells, the sounds . . . everything seems fresher and sharper. It's as if someone's dropped something naughty in your mint tea.

COOKING TAGINES
IN MARRAKECH

SI: On the drive into Marrakech from the airport, the huge red walls and gates of the city seem to stretch for miles. The mopeds flash around you, the donkey carts with their ten-year-old drivers lurch and sway past and everyone seems to be simultaneously greeting old friends and trying to run them over.

At the heart of Marrakech is the Djemaa el Fna, a huge, bustling square that acts as a kind of open-air theatre for every bit of madness you can imagine. Drummers, storytellers, false-teeth sellers, acrobats and food stalls. Although there are some slightly startled tourists wandering through the mayhem, this is a real local marketplace, not just for goods, but for experiences as well. There's more life and excitement in those few hundred square metres than in half a dozen holiday resorts stuck together.

One of the first things that happened was that a snake charmer took a shine to Myers and kept lifting a king cobra on and off his head. And as Dave was wearing a hat, he couldn't tell whether the snake was there or not. 'Kingy, is that a snake on me head or a hat?' has to be one of the weirder questions he's asked me over the years.

Street food in Morocco is extraordinary and the Djemaa el Fna square is the place to go for it. As night falls, the food stalls come out. Some are plain, like the stall selling just hard-boiled eggs, while others sell bucketfuls of snails poached in broth, kebabs, sausages and the highly prized sheep's head cooked on a spit. Now, you are pretty safe in Morocco

'We loved Marrakech, and the Djemaa el Fna in particular. So much so, that we had the daft idea of trying to cook a tagine in the middle of the square.' DAVE

with street food, but do look for stalls with lots of local clients (after all, they're not going to poison the regulars). Cooking will kill off most bugs, but if you can, get your food on a piece of paper, not a plate, because while the food may be fresh, the washing-up water sometimes isn't. I will leave you with one hot tip. Go to stall number fourteen for the best fish and chips in Morocco. I kid you not – they are sublime.

The food stalls in the Djemaa el Fna gave us our first taste of the richness of everyday Moroccan food. In fact, one of the best meals we had on our whole trip was at a garage. We'd stopped for fuel and realized that, instead of an old fridge boasting a couple of pies and a shelf of Coke, there was a simple outdoor restaurant full of Moroccans eating lunch en famille. The reason soon became clear. In common with many places in Morocco, the restaurant had its own butcher, greengrocer, breadmaker and cook. So you get to choose the cut of meat you want, have it chopped or minced to your taste, select some vegetables and bread to accompany it, get everything all cooked up and . . . heaven. Oh, for one of those on the A68.

DAVE: We loved Marrakech, and the Djemaa el Fna in particular. So much so, that we had the daft idea of trying to cook a tagine in the middle of the square. Now, this is the equivalent of a couple of Moroccans setting up a roast-beef stall underneath Nelson's Column and we weren't at all sure how it would be received. But as it turned out, we needn't have worried. Watched by up to a hundred locals, it was a really good day, with everybody joining in the tasting at the end. This meant that there wasn't much left for Kingy, but for once even that didn't stop him grinning.

BIKING

SI: For this trip, the bikes were shipped from the UK to Marrakech and all we had to do was meet them there. We had secured two BMW R1200 GS bikes and though we didn't seem to have too much off-road to do, the bikes arrived with knobblies (special tyres) just in case (our trips tend to develop a life of their own, so you can never tell).

Our first impressions of riding the bikes through Marrakech were very positive. Cyclists, taxis, buses, donkeys, mopeds and the odd camel constantly cut you up, but all with a smile and an apology, even from the camels. The main road network is good and the surfaces mostly tarmac (although there is some fantastic off-road biking to be had, should you wish to take up the challenge). And Dave and I both agreed that the run over the High Atlas Mountains from Marrakech was some of the finest motorcycling anywhere in the world. Each twist and turn up through the mountain passes revealed an even more beautiful vista than the last and the BMWs relished the roads, powering easily through the tight bends. The smiles beamed from the inside of our helmets prompted the cameraman to cheekily ask if we were shooting a toothpaste commercial.

We rode up into the mountains in January and although the roads were clear of snow, there were shadowy patches of ice on the bends. The 'dark bends', as we later called them, were treacherous because if you hit one and lose control, then you're up next on the tagine menu of the village seven hundred metres below. And there really is nothing to stop you shedding yourself over the side. Both Dave and I had an experience with the ice, but fortunately Dave was able to run along the only piece of Armco barrier this side of Casablanca, escaping with a scratched side panel and a twisted foot. The whole scenario could have been – how shall we say it? – more permanent.

Another very real hazard we encountered while driving in the mountains (and elsewhere) was the attitude that sticking to the middle of the road was better than either side. The obvious problem in the mountains when you meet such a driver is that the roads are narrow and so your choices are either a quick descent over the side or a rock wall. No matter how safe your riding line is, do be prepared at some point to stand the bike up in a bend.

To avoid another danger, the livestock on the roads, it's worth studying a day in the life of a Moroccan shepherd. 'What?' I hear you cry. Well, it's important and I'll tell you why. When you're out and about, you will see shepherds sitting with their backs to the road, watching their flocks. It seems that Moroccan livestock are an unruly bunch and have a penchant for running into the road, terrifying locals and tourists alike, so the authorities have decreed that the man or woman in charge of the herds will be in big trouble if they allow their animals to cause an accident. Good idea, you may think. However, the law only has effect during the day, and at dusk (the most difficult time to judge speed and distance) they are allowed to use the side of the road to drive their animals back home. It is mayhem, to the point where you really do not want to travel any quicker than forty kilometres an hour or you're likely to end up supplying the local restaurant with enough food for a feast.

Night riding is another pastime to be avoided if you can. I was told there's a law in Morocco that states vehicles travelling at less than twenty kilometres per hour do not need to have lights. Well, that's all well and good if you're a donkey or a camel, but most taxis and cars are so knackered that the law applies to them too. So it's total darkness right up to the point where you're drinking mint tea with the driver, converting to Islam and discussing the pros and cons of the nearest mosque. Hey ho, that's what we all love about biking.

SKIING IN THE
ATLAS MOUNTAINS

DAVE: Anyway, it was time to get on the bikes and head south from Marrakech. The next morning we set off towards the formidable Atlas Mountains, which sit like a snow-covered wall on the horizon beyond the city. There's always something about riding into mountains that gets the adrenaline going and riding over the Atlas was something we'd always dreamed about. We weren't disappointed. The palms and irrigation ditches around Marrakech gave way to scrub and cactus, and then to towering rock faces and tiny terraces. We lunched in a café above a gorge, trying each other's tagine and mopping up the gravy with fresh, warm bread. Then it was back on the bikes and up, round hairpin after hairpin, heading towards something Si hadn't really bargained for: a ski resort.

'You're having a laugh . . . aren't you?' said Mr King. Well, no. You see, I've always enjoyed skiing, though I hadn't done it for years. Kingy, on the other hand, thought that sliding down a mountain on a couple of planks was about as natural as the winner of a Miss Botox competition. His head was full of dunes, camels and Lawrence of Arabia, and here I was suggesting he'd be much happier slithering down the slopes like some kind of uncontrollable Geordie yeti. It wasn't going to happen. As we reached our destination, Oukaimeden, I realized it might not happen for me either. Whether it was global warming or just bad luck, there was not a lot of snow.

Luckily, there were a couple of runs with a decent covering, so it was off to get kitted out. However, not for this intrepid skier was there the extravagance of an alpine ski shop, racks of expensive skis and boots begging to be chosen. Nope, in Oukaimeden there's a pile of early '80s boots in the mud at the bottom of the slopes, available in at least three sizes (all wrong). And add to that a couple of cheery blokes thrusting skis at you that were last used by the Heroes of Telemark. But who cares? As we always say, just give it a go.

> **'His head was full of dunes, camels and Lawrence of Arabia, and here I was suggesting he'd be much happier slithering down the slopes like some kind of uncontrollable Geordie yeti.'** DAVE

So, while Si started preparing a big vat of harira, the Moroccan soup that makes you glow like the boy in the Ready-brek advert, I got on with my Franz Klammer impressions. 'Klammer?' yelled Kingy, 'Frodo, more like.' It's true that my djellaba (a full-length robe with a natty pointed hood) was perhaps more Hobbiton than the Hannenkahm, but then what does he know about style and grace?

SI: Watching Myers skidding down the slope made me realize the pain skiing can cause. I mean, when you're laughing that hard, it really can hurt. Dave looked like some kind of pneumatic Yoda who'd somehow got lost from a performance of Star Wars on Ice. Never mind, by the time he'd finished terrorizing the locals, the soup was well under way.

DAVE: Kingy toiled while I had a ball and skied like a loony. I then, I have to admit, ate the best, heartiest soup I had ever tasted, served up by Si, who, in his pale blue kaftan, mirror shades and bandanna, looked like a cross between Mama Cass and a break-dancing kebab-shop owner.

SI: The ride back down the other side of the Atlas was, if anything, even more inspiring. The hairpins and twisties near the top gradually uncoiled themselves into great long sweeps down the mountain, where for the first time we could let the bikes go a bit.

At a coffee shop in the town of El Kelaâ M'Gouna on our route, we learnt about a beautiful place called the Hidden Rose Valley, up in the mountains near Tourbist. The roses wouldn't be out till the spring, but we were told how stunning the location was, and how friendly the people up there were. It had to be done.

A FEAST AND A BIT OF BELLY DANCING

DAVE: What we hadn't been told was quite how gobsmackingly insane the road to the village was. Actually, let's drop the word 'road'; the 'track' to our destination bore the same resemblance to a road as Si does to Leonardo DiCaprio. After a long, long hour, we rumbled into the tiny Berber village of Tamaloute. Lights appeared from a little auberge and we staggered in to warm ourselves round a brazier and get Si to bed. The brazier followed us into the long, main room of the inn where we fell upon the soup, stews, couscous, fresh bread and fruit like men possessed.

That night, the temperature plummeted to a few degrees above freezing inside our lovely (if unheated) rooms, reminding us that we were still very much in the Atlas Mountains. However, the next morning brought one of those breakfasts you can spend a cold, sleepless night dreaming about. Hot, sweet mint tea, unleavened bread quickly fried on a griddle, eggs, fruit, honey and strong, dark coffee. But the best news was that Houssine, our host, was going to cook us a whole lamb, a mechoui, Morocco's great feast dish.

At dawn, a fire had been lit in a special clay oven a bit like a giant tandoor. Meanwhile, the lamb was killed, put on a spit made from moist fig wood and the meat rubbed down with ground ginger, cumin, cinnamon, garlic and oil. Now, when the oven is hot, a pan of water is placed in the bottom (the steaming water keeps the meat moist) and the spitted lamb lowered in vertically. The top and sides of the oven are sealed tight using a bucketful of wet clay, the chef like a plasterer as he watches for wisps of leaking smoke, slapping on clay to plug shut any holes. Once he was happy, the mechoui was left for a couple of hours, the cooking aromas filling the air. The whole process reminded me of a giant version of those Habitat chicken bricks everyone seems to have tucked away in a cupboard.

Meanwhile, someone made a heap of Berber bread, which looked like giant naan breads, the size of small duvets. The mechoui is carried to the table with great ceremony, adding to the feeling that you are about to eat something special. And we weren't disappointed – high in the mountains, food doesn't get much better than this.

SI: Now, a mechoui is a real feast, a special treat. So it seemed only right that we should invite round a few

of the locals and make a bit of an event out of it. Before we knew it, Houssine had got the word out and the local musicians and dancers arrived. It was a fascinating experience. The men and women lined up in two rows and gradually circled each other. The rhythms built, the voices rose higher and louder, and when some misguided soul handed me a drum, I couldn't help but join in.

There were only two problems. How were we going to reciprocate all Houssine's hospitality and where the hell was Dave? The answer to both was soon horribly apparent as I was forced to introduce 'The Flookburgh Fatima', otherwise known as a semi-naked, belly-dancing Myers. He launched himself onto the terrace with a glitter ball in his navel and a tray of lit candles on his head, looking like some nightmarish escapee from a video by The Cure. I'm not sure the nipple tassles were a great idea either, although he did manage to get them going in opposite directions at least once. The local guests coped with Dave's performance extremely well, although if a Berber village had such a thing as a psychotherapist, he or she'd probably be booked up till 2010.

Much as we loved the mountains, by now we were hearing the call of another mad piece of geography. Only a few hundred kilometres away was that massive bit of the map that always looks like they've forgotten to fill it in: the Sahara. And going across our bit of the Sahara, if we timed it right, was something we'd always dreamt of seeing: the Lisbon Dakar Rally. Catching this was one of our main motivations for coming on the trip and the thought of seeing those two-wheeled gladiators compete in one of the world's toughest enduro races was filling the two of us with more excitement than the prospect of a bacon sarnie.

THE LISBON DAKAR RALLY

DAVE: So we said goodbye to the mountains and headed east towards the town of Erfoud. And from there, we were assured, it was an easy ride to Merzouga, right on the edge of the Sahara. Easy in the daytime if you knew the way perhaps, but as it was, we found ourselves lost in a village in the dark while a group of very excited kids pointed us towards Merzouga. Only problem was that they were giving us their route, on foot across the dunes, not on great big BMWs weighing a quarter of a ton each. It wasn't nice. We staggered into our hotel and felt like John Mills ordering his beer in **Ice Cold in Alex**. God, it tasted good. And the next one.

The next day we staggered out of the rear of the hotel into a Saharan dawn. Huge silver dunes rolled towards us under a sky of red, purple, orange and gold. It really was like no dawn we'd ever seen. That morning we tried our hand at camel riding, though the lack of gears and a decent set of brakes did confuse Kingy somewhat.

Our poor camels, Bob Marley and Jimi Hendrix no less, must have been wondering whom they'd upset to end up with us two on top of them. But while we mucked about in the world's biggest sandpit, our reason for being there was getting closer. The Lisbon Dakar, formerly the Paris Dakar, is probably the most gruelling rally in the world. Bikes, cars and lorries thrash themselves to the limit across fifteen stages, and there's little doubt that the Moroccan sections are among the hardest.

SI: So it was that at 5.30 the next morning, as the sun rose over the starting gate and the crew stomped their feet to get warm, Myers and I looked at each other and grinned. Biker after biker launched themselves over the starting line, their smiles and relaxation disappearing in an explosion of dust, petrol and raw power. You couldn't fail to be moved by the dedication and bravery of these guys. They were spending two weeks absolutely on the edge of the possible, and your heart went out to every one of them. It was a fitting adventure to end our adventure, in a country we'd really grown to love.

'You know what, Kingy, I think we should have a go at this one year,' said Myers. That's when I knew he'd had too much sun.

On the other hand . . .

'"You know what, Kingy, I think we should have a go at this one year," said Myers. That's when I knew he'd had too much sun.' SI

THE FOOD

DAVE: Moroccan food is so special because it's all about home cooking. By that I mean that it's not like Turkish food, with a thousand tiny amuse-bouches fit for a sultan or a French chef's single poached langoustine, topped with watercress foam and a pea. It's about the kind of cooking that your mama does best, and this goes right through from the streets to the royal kitchens of Fez. The food may be homespun, but it is also very fine in its execution, using the freshest ingredients from Morocco's wonderful markets. Only a handful of spices are used, but this limited palette is employed with imagination.

Moroccan life is centred around the home and the sharing of meals is one of the most important pillars of society, bonding the strong sense of family and tribe. Women are mistresses of the home and hearth and they do most of the cooking, with even the grandest of hotels having a battalion of Moroccan ladies cooking away in their kitchens.

Although most men don't cook, they all seem to have an interest in food and are very vocal if something is not up to scratch – a bit like Si. They say in Morocco that a woman expresses her feelings through cooking and that a sensitive man should be able to judge her mood by subtle differences in his food. Perhaps just that touch more cumin indicates that 'er indoors needs a shelf putting up. Cor blimey! Imagine putting this to the test in some houses here. 'Ooh,' thinks Fred as he tastes his wife's shepherd's pie and sinks his top set into a mouthful of rusty nails, 'something's up with Fanny.'

THE TAGINE

The tagine is basically a casserole cooked in a special terracotta pot. The conical shape of the pot allows vapours from the simmering stew to evaporate and run back down so that the dish is constantly cooking in its own liquid and no precious flavours escape. It's the Colditz of cooking pots. Tagines range from a tiddly little one for a single person to a cement-mixer-sized one to feed a dozen diners. People sit around and eat straight from the pot, mopping up the tasty stew with warm bread.

When we rode through the Atlas Mountains, delicious cooking smells started to waft through our helmets as early as ten o'clock in the morning from the tagines that sit in smoking braziers outside each restaurant. Leave it another hour and the smells are getting stronger and more seductive as the spices marry with the meat. By twelve o'clock, that's all the torture you can take. You get off the bike and charge in. Almost before you are seated, the tagine is on the table with a mountain of fresh bread and you have a meal fit for a King . . . or indeed a Myers.

'The food may be homespun, but it is also very fine in its execution, using the freshest ingredients from Morocco's wonderful markets. Only a handful of spices are used, but this limited palette is employed with imagination' DAVE

You can put whatever you like into a tagine (lamb, chicken and vegetables are the most common ingredients), leave it to smoulder for a few hours and you'll generally come up trumps. Be adventurous. Our lamb with strawberries, mint and balsamic vinegar is a winner. The tagine is also great for cooking cheaper cuts of meat. Shin of beef is delicious and you can make a kind of osso bucco or Irish stew. To prepare the meat for a tagine, leave it on the bone because the marrow and cartilage cook down to thicken the stew. The Berbers say to brown lamb using a mixture of half olive and half sunflower oil, and for chicken use just olive oil. Then start building, layering the meat and veg as you wish. I like onions on the bottom so they caramelize and go sticky. The spices are usually based around the Big Five: cinnamon, ginger, cumin, coriander and saffron. Add a minimal quantity of either stock or water. This is important. The tagine is a rich, sticky beast, not a gravy fest.

'Put on your yellow curly-toed slippers and you'll feel just like a sultan.'
DAVE

As you will have gathered by now, I'm a big fan of the tagine. I love coming home at about six o'clock, taking just ten minutes to peel some vegetables, add a few spices and build the tagine. Leave it to cook for a couple of hours, filling your house with cooking smells, then when you're good and hungry, take your pot to the table and enjoy. Put on your yellow curly-toed slippers and you'll feel just like a sultan. If you're having friends over, why not cook one with just vegetables, one with, say, lamb and almonds, and a nice duck one. Let them simmer all afternoon and when your guests arrive all you, the creative genius in the kitchen, have to do is bring the pots to the table.

COUSCOUS

I once had a friend who had a cat called Couscous (and another called Falafel). She had a liking for multicoloured jumpers and ran a Citroën 2CV on All Bran. But couscous doesn't have to be the worthy preserve of yoghurt knitters. It is fab.

Couscous is a semolina, just like our fine pudding semolina but left chunky. Instant couscous is easily available and our method for preparing it can be found in this book (the traditional method is much more laborious and, to be honest, I'm not sure it's worth the effort). If you make your couscous with stock and some butter or olive oil, it's really good. Try adding sun-dried tomatoes or some porcini mushrooms. The choice is yours. Couscous is also great for stuffing a chicken because as the bird cooks, the couscous absorbs all the chicken juices.

MOROCCAN PASTRY

The complicated gastronomic flagship of the Moroccan kitchen is the pastilla. We had to go back to school to find out how to make it and our recipe comes from what we learnt in the hands of top chefs Aziza and Mohammed. Pastilla is like a giant Eccles cake, a light, filo-like pastry, traditionally filled with pigeon breast, almond paste and eggs and topped with cinnamon and icing sugar. Arrgh, I feel that I'm not doing a very good job of selling this one to you. It is special and well worth a taste, though nowadays it is often done with chicken.

A pastilla should be round and the one I made was like the finely balanced wheel off a Formula One car, such was the symmetry and balance. Kingy's was like an old thrupenny bit, with more sides than a Rubik's Cube. I have to say, though, that when cooked they both tasted absolutely delicious. The pastilla epitomizes Moroccan cuisine in its mixture of textures and spices, both sweet and savoury.

Another Moroccan pastry that we learnt to love is the briouat. The briouat is a kind of samosa filled with fish, meat, chicken or cheese and honey. They are either tiny and triangular in shape or like a small spring roll. Traditionally spiced, we found that they make a wonderful starter and are so moreish that you need to take care or you won't finish your tagine, chuck!

'Couscous doesn't have to be the worthy preserve of yoghurt knitters. It is fab.' DAVE

FRUIT, PRESERVES AND OLIVES

Because of its warm climate, Morocco is a fruit lover's paradise. Oranges, grapefruits and lemons are grown year round and one of Marrakech's gastronomic highlights is the chilled, freshly squeezed orange juice found in the Djemaa el Fna. Dates, melons, apples, plums, apricots, pomegranates, figs and grapes are all grown and so desserts in Morocco are usually a fruit salad of some kind.

The Moroccans are great at making jams and preserves. Quince jelly is everywhere and there are also brilliant preserved lemons. These are now readily available in the UK or you can make your own. Preserved lemons can be mixed with lamb or chicken in tagines. The Berbers use only the lemon rind with lamb and the pulp with chicken, but I think this is just being picky. The lemons can also be used as a salad, chopped very finely and served in a yellow mound, or I really love sprinkling them over a simple piece of grilled fish. Ooh, they're lovely.

Moroccan olives are among the best to be found anywhere in the Mediterranean and are often flavoured with cumin, chilli, thyme or paprika. The extra virgin olive oil here is also first class. Moroccan salads are heavy with it and it is a mighty fine thing to use as a dip for home-made bread. Another oil that Morocco is famous for is the miraculous argan oil. Although nothing to do with Jason and his Argonauts, it is an oil of myth and legend. Made from the nuts of the argan tree, it is used as a dipping oil and sometimes mixed with almonds and honey to make amlou, a spread that is amazing on pancakes or bread. The oil has a gentle nutty scent – it's lovely.

SPICES

The varieties of spices available in Morocco are a bit limited, but I think this is a good thing. The food has a distinct identity and the flavours never get muddy.

1. The number one spice is **ground cumin**. This is in everything and is always on the table alongside the salt to be sprinkled over your meal. It is used as a rub with meat and in all tagines.

2. At number two, pop pickers, comes **ground ginger**. This puts some zip in your pip and a tang in your tagine. It's warm and exotic and is always used in its powdered form in Morocco.

3. Closely following at number three is powdered **cinnamon**. Here cinnamon is not just for your apple pie. It gives us the sweet in Morocco's sweet-and-sour cooking and is an enduring theme in soups and tagines. It is lovely sprinkled over an orange for a simple dessert.

4. Number four is the emperor of spice: **saffron**. For me, Moroccan saffron is the best, more intense than Turkish or Iranian. A pinch is all that is required to colour and flavour food.

5. Number five is **ground coriander**, which is used alongside **ground cumin** with meat and in tagines.

6. Fresh **flat-leaf parsley** and **coriander** are added liberally towards the end of the cooking time, Moroccans obey that old rule of cooking the dry spices in the dish and adding the fresh ones close to the end, with the effect that Moroccan dishes have many different levels of flavour.

7. If you come to Morocco, do make sure to buy some **ras-el-hanout**. Translated, this means 'shopkeeper's choice' and is a universal, go-in-anything spice that can have up to thirty-five different ingredients (though most have around thirteen). It contains all the aforementioned spices, but also things like mace, thyme, cardamoms, lavender and rose petals. This spice mix would appear to contradict what I said about keeping things pure and simple, but ras-el-hanout is like the signature scent of a perfumer – no two are alike. As a customer, you tend to find one you like and stick to it. I bought a pot from Ali who runs Epices Avenzoar in the medina in Marrakech and have already mixed it with yoghurt to make a brilliant marinade for barbecued meats. It will be a firm favourite for as long as it lasts.

HARIRA   MAKES 6-8 HEARTY PORTIONS

This soup is very important to the Moroccans. Before you eat your meal, you always have an option of a soup or salad to start with, and the soup is nearly always harira. During Ramadan, you eat the soup for breakfast with sweet dates before dawn and then, as night falls, you use the soup to break the day's fast. The recipe varies from family to family, but it commonly starts with a hearty meat stock, veg, spices, pulses and rice or pasta, or both. We cooked ours in the snow and very fine it was too.

300g rump steak, finely chopped
4 tablespoons olive oil
1 onion, chopped
2 sticks of celery, chopped
2 carrots, chopped
100g red lentils
100g green lentils
100g rice
2 cloves of garlic, crushed
1 teaspoon ground cinnamon
a large pinch of saffron

3 teaspoons ground cumin
400g tin of chickpeas
400g tin of chopped tomatoes
2 litres beef stock
100g vermicelli
150g French beans,
  cut into 1cm lengths
juice of ½ lemon
a bunch of fresh coriander, chopped
a bunch of fresh flat-leaf
  parsley, chopped

Firstly, brown the meat over a high heat in 2 tablespoons of the olive oil, then take out and set aside.

In the same pan, cook the onion, celery and carrot over a lower heat for 5 minutes until tender but not coloured. Also remove from the pan and set aside.

Add the lentils, rice, garlic, cinnamon, saffron and cumin to the pan and stir to coat the whole lot in the remaining olive oil.

Stir in the chickpeas, tomatoes, stock and the reserved meat and vegetables and bring to the boil. Cover and simmer for 25 minutes.

After 25 minutes, add the vermicelli and the French beans. After a further 5 minutes' cooking, squeeze in the lemon juice and add the coriander and parsley.

Serve the soup with warm bread, a plate of dates on the side or a little bowl of harissa. Eat this, then go and chop down a tree or conquer Everest.

CARROT, ROASTED RED PEPPER AND CUMIN SALAD   SERVES 4–6

A see-in-the-dark salad, this is more orange than an Essex girl's tan.

500g carrots, roughly chopped
2 red peppers
1 teaspoon ground cumin
2 cloves of garlic, finely chopped
juice of ½ lemon

½ teaspoon harissa or
  more if you like it hot
3 tablespoons olive oil
a small handful of fresh parsley,
  finely chopped

Cook the carrot in a pan of boiling salted water for 10 minutes until soft.

Roast the peppers over a gas flame for about 10 minutes, turning them with tongs, or put in a 200°C oven for 15 minutes until they blister. Take them out of the oven or away from the heat and put in a plastic bag or a bowl covered with clingfilm for 10 minutes. Once the peppers are cool enough to handle, remove the skins and the seeds and roughly chop.

While the carrot is still hot, mash or blend to a rough paste, then add the cumin, garlic, lemon juice, harissa, olive oil and roasted peppers. Mash or blend to mix in these ingredients. Finally, fold in the parsley and serve as part of a salad table or on its own with bread.

SALAD ZAALOUK, OR MOROCCAN AUBERGINE SALAD SERVES 6

This is a great robust salad, which can be part of a salad table or served on its own as an appetizer. It's tasty and zingy and, with the preserved lemon, has a lovely tang. Keep it quite chunky because it isn't meant to be a dip or purée.

2 aubergines, cut lengthways
  into 1cm slices
7 tablespoons olive oil
3 large juicy tomatoes
24 black olives, stoned
½ teaspoon sugar
3 cloves of garlic, crushed
1 teaspoon ground cumin

½ teaspoon paprika
juice of ½ lemon
1 small preserved lemon,
  finely chopped
a good handful of chopped
  fresh coriander leaves
a good handful of chopped
  fresh flat-leaf parsley

Preheat the oven to 200°C.

Place the aubergine in a single layer on a flat baking tray (you may need to cook them in batches). Drizzle 2 tablespoons of the olive oil over them and bake for about 20 minutes until golden brown. Leave to cool, then roughly chop.

Remove the eye from the tomatoes, place in a bowl and pour over boiling water. Leave to stand for 10 to 15 seconds before draining. Peel away the skin, take out the seeds and chop.

Place the aubergine in a large mixing bowl and add all the other ingredients. Mix it up till it goes a bit gloopy, mashing the ingredients together slightly, but remembering it's not a purée. Season to taste.

You can leave the salad for a couple of hours for the flavours to intensify. Garnish with a drizzle of olive oil, more parsley and a sprinkling of sea salt flakes. Ooh, take me to the kasbah, Fatima.

POMEGRANATE AND CHICKPEA SALAD

SERVES 4–6

This salad looks like the inside of a tart's handbag, but contains all the colours and sensations of the mysterious East. Break out your tinted visor for this one – you'll need it!

2 x 400g tins of chickpeas,
  drained and rinsed

seeds of 2 pomegranates

4 oranges, peeled and segmented
  (see page 33), retaining the juice

1 red onion, finely chopped

1 large handful of
  chopped fresh mint

6–8 tablespoons olive oil

Stir all the ingredients together in a big bowl with a good pinch of salt and some ground black pepper. Get your hands in and mix well.

Leave in the fridge for a minimum of half an hour before eating. It's even better the following day.

That's it. How simple is that? It tastes bloody lovely and looks great.

PRAWNS WITH PAPRIKA AND HONEY

SERVES 4 AS A STARTER OR 2 AS A MAIN

This is a great spicy dish that you won't be able to stop eating. Morocco has an amazing coastline, so you get a wonderful variety of shellfish. Use whatever sort of prawns you like, just buy the best and always raw. We never understand why, oh why, supermarkets only seem to stock boiled prawns. Wake up! We have all come a long way since the only place for a prawn was in a cocktail.

50g butter
4 tablespoons olive oil
3 shallots, finely chopped
1 green chilli, seeded
  and thinly sliced
3 cloves of garlic, thinly sliced
a thumb-sized piece of ginger

1 teaspoon paprika
500g peeled raw tiger prawns
4 large shell-on raw prawns
2 tablespoons runny honey
a small handful of
  chopped fresh parsley
lemon wedges, to serve

In a large pan, melt the butter with the olive oil and fry the shallot over a medium high heat until translucent.

Add the chilli, garlic and ginger and cook for a further 2 minutes. Add the paprika and all the prawns and cook over a medium heat for 3 to 5 minutes until the prawns are pink. Remove from the heat before finally adding the honey to glaze the prawns.

At the last minute, add the parsley and season to taste. Finish off with a few lemon wedges.

Serve the prawns with some funky bread and salad as a starter or with simple basmati as a main course. This is absolute prawnography!

SQUID WITH HARISSA AND ORANGE SAUCE

SERVES 4 AS A STARTER AND 2 AS A MAIN COURSE

A Moroccan take on a Mediterranean classic, this is great to eat, has so few calories and looks the dog's when served to your gathered guests. Hoorah, we hear the pans clanking all over Notting Hill.

1kg squid

1 onion, chopped

2 teaspoons harissa (available at most supermarkets or see our recipe)

6 spring onions, sliced at a jaunty angle

2 mild red chillies, seeded and sliced into thin strips

juice of 2 oranges and zest of 1, to garnish

2 teaspoons ground cumin

1 teaspoon ground cinnamon

rocket leaves, to serve

3 tablespoons olive oil

Separate the tube from the rest of the squid, remove the outer and inner membranes, then pull the quill from the inside of the tube (it looks like a bit of plastic and acted as the squid's backbone when the poor thing was alive).

Open up the tube so it looks like a square of white rubber (hopefully this is not how it will end up). Score the fleshy inside with a criss-cross pattern, making sure you don't cut through (or get the fishmonger to do it if you can't be arsed). As the squid cooks, the crosshatching will hold your sauce and make the squid curl nicely.

Heat the oil in a pan over a medium-high heat and cook the onion until translucent. Add the harissa, spring onion and chilli to the pan and cook for 1 minute.

Add the squid to the pan over a medium-high heat and cook for no more than a minute (any longer and it will be tough). Remove the squid and transfer to a warm plate.

To the pan that the squid has been cooked in, add the orange juice, cumin and cinnamon and boil for a minute, then remove from the heat.

Return the squid to the pan, coating thoroughly with the sauce. Season to taste and serve on a bed of rocket dressed with a little olive oil (the peppery rocket complements the spicy orange sauce really well).

Sprinkle over the orange zest as a garnish. If you like it a bit spicier, place an additional spoonful of harissa on the side.

CHEESE AND HONEY BRIOUATS

MAKES ABOUT 15

Briouats are little cigar-shaped Moroccan pastries, great with drinks or as a starter. These cheese and honey ones are superb with a glass of red wine and you can't stop eating them. Serve some of these and some of the spicy meat ones together. Yummy yum-yums.

4 tablespoons runny honey
250g soft goat's cheese,
  cut into tiny cubes or crumbled
1 (400g) packet of filo pastry

50g melted butter
1 egg yolk
vegetable oil, for deep-frying

Mix the honey with the cheese in a bowl.

Carefully lay out the filo pastry. Now, with the skill and dexterity of Michael Flatley's feet of flames, cut the pastry into 10 by 15cm strips.

Place a little sausage of the cheese and honey mixture in the middle of each strip. Coat the outside edges of the pastry with melted butter and, in the manner of a Cuban Madame rolling a Havana, roll the parcel up, tucking the sides in as you go. Seal the end flap with egg yolk.

Chill the pastries for an hour so they don't unravel when they're cooking. Heat a deep-fat fryer or large pan of oil to 180°C then deep-fry in the oil for 3 to 4 minutes or until they are golden.

A good idea would be to make a heap of the cheese and honey and the spicy meat briouats and freeze them. They could be cooked from frozen just in time for that special dinner party. Go on, create with confidence.

SPICY MEAT BRIOUATS   MAKES ABOUT 15

Fanny Craddock would be proud of us: finger food for when the vicar, priest, rabbi or haman pops in. Arrgh, let's get real, these are fantastic with a few cold beers and the chicks will love the cheese and honey ones (see previous recipe). No letters please, we are PC really.

1 tablespoon olive oil
1 onion, very finely chopped
250g steak mince
2 cloves of garlic, crushed
1 teaspoon ground cumin
a pinch of cayenne pepper

a pinch of ground ginger
3 eggs, beaten
1 (400g) packet of filo pastry
50g melted butter
1 egg yolk, beaten
vegetable oil, for deep-frying

Heat the olive oil in a frying pan and cook the onion over a medium heat for 6 to 9 minutes until translucent. Add the mince, garlic and the spices and cook until the meat is brown.

Add the eggs to the meat and remove the pan from the heat, moving them constantly until they are cooked. Add salt and pepper to taste and set aside to cool.

Carefully lay out the filo pastry. Cut into rectangles about 15cm in length and 10cm in width and brush all over one side of the pastry with the melted butter.

Place a small sausage of the mixture halfway down each rectangle and about 2cm from either edge of the pastry. Fold over the pastry edges so they partially cover your filling, then roll the short end over and continue to roll to the end of your pastry so you form small, spring roll-shaped parcels.

Before you finish rolling, brush the end of the pastry with the beaten egg yolk to help seal the rolls as they are frying.

Set aside your rolled lovelies on a baking tray and chill in the fridge for half an hour. Heat a deep-fat fryer to about 180°C or heat a saucepan of oil on your hob. When it is very hot, cook the briouats for 4 to 5 minutes or until golden brown.

HARISSA   MAKES A JARFUL

Harissa isn't Moroccan, you know, it's Tunisian. However, it has become part and parcel of Moroccan cuisine. We love this flavoursome spicy sauce with a meat tagine, fish, or indeed with, well, almost anything really. It's Moroccan ketchup.

1 teaspoon caraway seeds

2 teaspoons coriander seeds

1 red pepper

200g large red chillies

5 large cloves of garlic, peeled and crushed

¼ preserved lemon, finely chopped

½ teaspoon smoked paprika

2 teaspoons ground cumin

1 tablespoon tomato purée

juice of ½ lemon

8 tablespoons olive oil

In a dry frying pan, dry roast the caraway and coriander seeds until they start to pop. This releases the flavour and natural oils.

Roast the pepper over a gas flame for about 10 minutes, turning it with tongs, or put in a 200°C oven for 15 minutes until it blisters. Take it out of the oven or away from the heat and put in a plastic bag or a bowl covered with clingfilm for 10 minutes. Once the pepper is cool enough to handle, remove the skin and take out the seeds.

Cut the chillies into quarters and remove the seeds. Roast them in a dry frying pan for 5 minutes, moving constantly. Just to warn you, this is pretty torturous. Don't forget to wash your hands thoroughly after you've handled the chillies too.

Once you've roasted your chillies, put all the ingredients into a blender except the olive oil. Blend, add some salt, then add the oil gradually and blend slowly for 4 to 5 seconds until smooth. If it's still a little thick, add more oil.

Harissa can be stored for a month or so (always ready to spice up your life) in a jar with olive oil floated on the top.

CHICKEN TAGINE WITH PRESERVED LEMONS AND OLIVES   SERVES 4

The Moroccans are mad for really tasty, inventive stews and this tagine is one of the most commonly served. It's a great mix of slowly cooked chicken, tangy lemons, juicy olives and fragrant spices and it will make you smack your lips. This tagine would be great made the day before and left so that the flavours can infuse. If you haven't got a tagine, you can use a casserole dish or something similar.

½ teaspoon saffron (or more if you like), crushed

250ml chicken stock

3 onions, chopped

2–3 tablespoons olive oil

1 teaspoon ground ginger

1 teaspoon ground cumin

3 cloves of garlic, thinly sliced

1 (approximately 1kg) chicken, jointed (ask your butcher to do this or buy chicken portions)

1 teaspoon crushed black peppercorns

6 small preserved lemons, quartered or 2 chopped up big ones

100g mixed olives (green is traditional, but we like a mix)

a good handful of chopped fresh coriander leaves

a good handful of chopped fresh flat-leaf parsley

Put the saffron in the hot stock to infuse. Meanwhile, back at the tagine (or casserole dish), cook the onion in the olive oil over a low heat until soft. Add the ginger, cumin and garlic and cook gently for a couple of minutes. Add the chicken and stir to coat with the spicy onion lovelies.

Sprinkle on the crushed peppercorns, add the lemon and the saffron-infused stock (this dish is yellower than a jaundiced canary . . . but ten times as tasty) and bring to the boil.

Cover the tagine and cook over a very gentle heat for about 1 hour or so until the chicken is falling apart. Add the olives, season with salt and pepper and continue to simmer for another 10 minutes.

Just before serving, add the coriander and parsley so it wilts a bit, but isn't cooked to death. In Morocco they don't serve couscous with tagines, which we think is odd because they go together perfectly. As an alternative, try with potatoes, chunks of crusty bread or we think this one works really well with rice and a green salad.

COUSCOUS WITH CHICKEN   SERVES 6

In Morocco this would traditionally be cooked in a **couscoussier**, a large saucepan with a steamer on top for the couscous so that it cooks in the steam released by the meat and vegetables below. If you've got one, great, but if you haven't, cook the stew and the couscous separately. We prepare the couscous with chicken stock (see couscous recipe on page 242). If you want a vegetarian version, simply leave out the chicken and bring the couscous to life with vegetable stock. It's an all-in-one meal, this, and a real communal dish, where you eat together out of the same pot.

4 tablespoons olive oil

1 large chicken, jointed
  (ask your butcher to do this
  for you or buy chicken portions)

1 onion, cut chunky

3 carrots, sliced at an angle

1 stick of celery, chopped

½ tin of chickpeas

3 teaspoons ground cumin

a pinch of saffron

½ teaspoon paprika

2 small preserved lemons,
  finely chopped

3 tomatoes, cut into chunks

2 red peppers, chopped into
  large chunks

3 cloves of garlic, thinly sliced

3 courgettes, sliced at an angle

1 x couscous (see page 242)

In a large casserole dish with a lid, heat the oil over a medium-high heat and brown your chicken for 4 to 5 minutes on all sides. Once the chicken has browned, add the onion and cook for 6 to 7 minutes over a medium heat until softened.

Add the carrot, celery, chickpeas, cumin, saffron, paprika, lemon, tomato, red pepper and garlic. Put the lid on the dish, reduce the heat and cook for 20 minutes. Add the courgette and cook for a further 10 to 15 minutes.

To serve this dish, put the warm couscous in a buttered medium-sized bowl and press firmly down. Turn out the bowl on to a large plate and place the chicken pieces around the bottom of your couscous dome. Place the vegetables carefully on top of the couscous and spoon over some of the delicious cooking juices. Serve as a centrepiece and allow your guests to dig in and serve themselves. Give them side plates so they don't make a mess on your tablecloth.

PASTILLA SERVES 4

This is a very important dish in Morocco, one that is made for weddings and funerals. It's quite a complicated dish to cook, but worth the effort. Traditionally, it is done with pigeon, but this does end up being a bone and scraps of meat affair. You could make it with chicken, but we think that's a bit ordinary, so our pastilla uses duck breasts, which give us a rich flavour that supports all the spices and sweet and sour elements going on. For this dish we went back to school, joining the oldest cookery school in Morocco, the esteemed La Maison Arabe. We donned our pinnies, took notes and, hey up, turned out a Moroccan classic.

for the duck and egg filling
2 fat duck breasts
1 teaspoon salt
½ teaspoon ground black pepper
1 teaspoon ground ginger
1 cinnamon stick
a large pinch of saffron
½ onion, chopped
a small handful of chopped
  fresh coriander
a small handful of chopped
  fresh flat-leaf parsley
4 eggs

for the nut layer
125g blanched almonds
25g caster sugar
2 teaspoons melted butter
1 teaspoon ground cinnamon
1 teaspoon orange blossom water

12 large sheets of filo pastry
75g melted butter
1 egg, beaten
vegetable oil, for shallow frying
icing sugar and ground cinnamon,
  to decorate

Now, let battle commence. Place the duck breasts skin-side down in a small hot frying pan and sear until browned. As the duck produces fat, no extra fat is required.

Add the salt, pepper, ginger, cinnamon, saffron, onion, coriander and parsley. Cover with water and simmer for about half an hour until the liquid has reduced and the duck is cooked.

Meanwhile, heat a small frying pan over a medium to high heat and dry fry the almonds until golden. When the almonds are cool, place in a blender with the sugar, melted butter, cinnamon and the orange blossom water. Give it a short blast until the almonds are the texture of couscous and set aside.

Meanwhile, back with the duck, discard the duck skin and cinnamon and shred the meat with a fork. Reduce the liquid in the pan to roughly 4 tablespoons (a thinnish layer of juice in the base of the pan). Put the shredded meat back in the pan with the cooking juices and spices and take it off the heat. Add the eggs and scramble the whole lot together over a low, low heat. When set, set aside.

Now for the assembly. Each pastilla needs six sheets of filo (because we haven't got Moroccan pastry, we are using the more fragile filo and so will have to use two sheets for each layer).

To make the first pastilla, use a dinner plate as a template to cut out six circles of pastry from six sheets of filo. Take a side plate and place on the work surface. Lay a circle of the pastry over the plate so that it hangs evenly over the sides, brush with the melted butter then cover with a second circle of the pastry so that it is double thick. In the middle of the pastry circle, spread out half of the ducky egg mixture to the edge of the plate. Coat the naked pastry edges with the beaten egg and cover with another circle of pastry. Coat this top layer with butter then add another filo disc on top.

Now spread on half of the nut mixture the same way as you did the duck one. Paint the overlapping edges of pastry with the beaten egg and fold the edges to the centre, trying not to get too many corners. It will begin to look like a giant Eccles cake. Cut any excess pastry away with a pair of scissors.

Now for the athletic bit. Take the remaining two sheets of pastry and lay them on top of your pastilla with a layer of melted butter in between. Turn the whole thing over and remove the plate. Bring the edges of the pastry up and seal the parcel with beaten egg to make a very tidy Eccles cake. Now make the next pastilla with the remaining mixture.

Shallow fry the pastillas in a pan of hot vegetable oil until golden brown.

Sieve over the icing sugar (this makes it look even more like an Eccles cake) and sprinkle a grid shape over the top with cinnamon. There you have it, a Moroccan classic. Which way to the belly-dancing class?

KEFTA MQAWARA TAGINE
(MEATBALLS WITH EGGS ON TOP)   SERVES 4

This is an absolute winner that we guarantee will become part of your repertoire. Repeatedly in Morocco we found ourselves ordering this at restaurants and it makes superb comfort food, you can even dip soldiers into the baked eggs on top. It would be great with couscous or, let's face it, brilliant with chips (see the Belgium chapter). Try this with the kids – there are no mystery bits.

for the meatballs
500g minced beef or lamb
1 onion, very, very finely chopped
3 cloves of garlic, crushed
1 teaspoon ground ginger
1 teaspoon ground cumin
½ teaspoon chilli powder
1 teaspoon paprika
a small handful of finely
  chopped fresh coriander leaves
a small handful of finely
  chopped fresh flat-leaf parsley
1 egg yolk

for the sauce
2 tablespoons olive oil
1 small onion, finely chopped
2 tablespoons tomato purée
400g tin of chopped tomatoes,
  drained of excess juice
2 teaspoons honey
200g frozen peas
4 free-range eggs

chopped fresh parsley,
  to garnish

First, construct your meatballs. In a big bowl, mix together the beef, onion, garlic, spices, fresh herbs, egg yolk and some salt and pepper. Get your hands in it to knead this all together and form a smooth paste. Shape into walnut-sized balls and set aside.

In a tagine (or casserole dish), heat up the olive oil and cook the onion slowly over a low heat until translucent.

Add the meatballs and brown lightly over medium-high heat. Stir the tomato purée into the tomatoes and add to the tagine along with the honey. Cover and simmer for 10 minutes. Stir in the peas, then break the eggs on top of the stew, turn the heat right down and cook with the lid on until you have the eggs how you like them. We think baking them for about 10 minutes is just right, but if you want Edwina Currie bullet eggs, leave them for longer. Garnish with a little parsley and serve.

MOROCCAN LAMB PILAF SERVES 4

Fed up with couscous? Have a pilaf. Rice is used less in Morocco than in other countries, but there are still a few Middle-Eastern pilafs around. Pilafs are kind of like a risotto, but lighter and spicier. We use anchovies in ours. You won't know they're there, but they give the lamb a wonderful taste.

2 tablespoons olive oil
500g shoulder of lamb,
  very finely chopped
1 onion, very finely chopped
1 aubergine, very finely chopped
3 cloves of garlic, crushed
2 teaspoons ground cumin
½ teaspoon cayenne pepper
a good pinch of saffron

175g long-grain rice
750ml meat stock
  (beef, lamb or chicken)
1 large tomato, finely chopped
5 anchovy fillets, finely chopped
1 tablespoon roasted almonds,
  chopped
2 tablespoons currants
chopped fresh flat-leaf parsley,
  to garnish

Put the oil in a non-stick frying pan (one that has a lid) and sear the lamb over a high heat until it is brown all over. Add the onion, aubergine, garlic, cumin, cayenne and saffron, turn the heat down and cook slowly for around 5 minutes. Add the rice and stir until it is coated with the meat mixture.

Add the stock, tomato, anchovies, almonds and currants Stir, then cover and cook for around 15 minutes or until the rice is done. Season to taste at the end because the stock contains salt, as do the anchovies.

Scatter with the parsley and serve with a nice green salad.

LAMB AND STRAWBERRY TAGINE **SERVES 4–6**

This may sound like a bit of a whore's breakfast, but strawberry fields forever! It's the old fruit and meat again, but it really tastes good slow cooked and enjoyed with bread or couscous. Perfect for that summer dinner, served outside on the patio or in your shed down the allotment.

300g strawberries,
  hulled and quartered

4 teaspoons caster sugar

2 tablespoons balsamic vinegar

50g butter

4 tablespoons olive oil

1kg lamb, cut into chunks
  (shoulder is the one you want)

1 onion, finely chopped

6 shallots, peeled and halved

4 cloves of garlic, sliced

2 teaspoons ground cumin

4 sprigs of rosemary

100ml stock (whatever you fancy)

2 teaspoons dried mint,
  ground to a powder

a handful of fresh mint leaves,
  for garnish

In a bowl, mix the strawberries with the sugar and balsamic vinegar. Set aside in the fridge to marinate while the lamb cooks.

In a tagine or casserole dish, melt the butter in the oil over a medium high heat. When hot, add the lamb chunks and brown them (don't forget to do this in batches if necessary).

Remove the meat and set aside. In the same pan, cook the onion, shallots and garlic a little until the onion becomes soft. Return the meat to the pan.

Add the cumin, sprigs of rosemary, stock, dried mint and some seasoning. Cover and leave to simmer gently for about 2 hours.

Five minutes before the end of the cooking time, add the strawberries and marinade that you prepared earlier to your tagine.

Once cooked, add the fresh mint to garnish and serve with couscous, bread or roast tatties and a veg of your choice.

LAMB TAGINE WITH
PRUNES AND ALMONDS   SERVES 4–6

A traditional Moroccan tagine, but with a more savoury twist. This is quite a dry tagine, with falling-apart meat and sticky prunes that are fantastic with the lamb. The almonds give it a bit of crunch.

2 tablespoons olive oil
1kg shoulder of lamb,
  cut into big chunks
1 red onion, finely chopped
3 cloves of garlic, sliced
1 green chilli, seeded and chopped

2 small preserved lemons,
  finely chopped
2 teaspoons ground cumin
50g almonds
375g prunes, presoaked and stoned
2 tablespoons sesame seeds

Heat up the oil in a tagine or casserole dish and brown the lamb. Add the onion, garlic, chilli, preserved lemon and the cumin. Bring to the boil and then cover and simmer gently for an hour.

Meanwhile, in a dry frying pan, lightly toast the almonds.

Remove the dish from the heat and cover the lamb with a tidy layer of prunes, placed in a pattern of your choice. Top each prune with an almond and sprinkle the sesame seeds over the top.

Cover and return to the heat, bring back to a gentle simmer and cook for a further 15 minutes or until the prunes are soft and sticky.

Serve with pride. Delicious with roast potatoes and some greens.

HAKE WITH TAPENADE AND CARAMELIZED PEARS   SERVES 4

It's easy to forget that Morocco has a huge coastline, that along with its mountains, cities and the Sahara, there is the seaside with all the food and culture that is attached to that. This recipe is great with cod, hake or any white fish, the tapenade balancing the sweetness of the pears.

for the tapenade

150g black olives, stoned

25g capers

6 anchovies

6 cloves of garlic, roughly chopped

1 teaspoon fresh thyme leaves, chopped

2 tablespoons extra-virgin olive oil

a good grind of black pepper

for the fish and caramelized pears

2 tablespoons olive oil

50g butter

2 tablespoons caster sugar

½ teaspoon ground cinnamon

½ teaspoon ground cumin

4 teaspoons balsamic vinegar

4 ripe pears, peeled, cored and quartered

4 nice hake steaks

a squeeze of lemon juice

250ml natural yoghurt

2 tablespoons shredded fresh basil

lemon, to garnish

To make the tapenade, purée all the ingredients together in a food processor. Then, in a large frying pan with a lid, heat 2 teaspoons of the oil and the butter together (the oil is to stop the butter burning). Add the sugar, cinnamon, cumin and balsamic vinegar. Add a sprinkle of black pepper at this stage. When the sugar has dissolved, add the pear and cook, covered, for about 15 minutes over a super-low heat until golden and soft. Putting the lid back on will help prevent the sugar from burning, but do keep your eye on it anyway. Set the pear aside.

Massage the hake with the remaining olive oil and the lemon juice and place in a hot, dry non-stick frying pan. Cook over high heat for about 1 minute each side, then reduce the heat and cook for about 5 minutes on each side until browned, but not burnt.

Bring the pears back to a simmer and add the yoghurt. Cook for 1 minute, taking care not to overcook or the sauce will split. At the last minute, add the basil. To serve, spoon the pears on to four plates and top with a fish steak and spoonful of tapenade. Garnish with lemon wedges.

MEDFOUNA   SERVES 4

After a night in the desert, we cooked this for our breakfast. A bit of comfort food, it's a bit like a cross between a stuffed naan and a toasted sandwich on steroids. Go on, give it a go.

for the bread
250g plain flour
a sachet (7g) of dried yeast
1 teaspoon caraway seeds
½ teaspoon salt
olive oil
sea salt

for the filling
500g fillet steak
1 onion, finely chopped
½ large stick of celery,
  finely chopped
2 tablespoons chopped fresh thyme
4 tablespoons chopped fresh
  flat-leaf parsley
1 teaspoon ground coriander
1 tablespoon olive oil

To make the dough, place the flour in a bowl. Add the yeast to 175ml blood-temperature (lukewarm) water and mix to dissolve. Stir the caraway and salt into the flour to distribute the seeds. Add the yeast water and mix to form a dough. On a floured work surface, knead the dough for a good 10 minutes. There is no better way to make yourself feel good than to make bread and it's not just for the ladies either, so get stuck in, lads, it's great.

Divide the dough into two and place in two bowls. Cover the bowls with tea towels or clingfilm and leave to rise in a warm, draught-free place for half an hour or so until the dough has doubled in size.

Now, get cracking with the filling while your masterpiece is rising. Finely chop your fillet steak into very small pieces, but don't mince it. Add the onion, celery, thyme, parsley, coriander and olive oil and mix through the meat. Add salt and pepper to taste and set aside to wait for your dough.

Preheat the oven to 180°C.

Once your dough has risen, roll out both portions into large rounds the size of a dinner plate (or any shape you want really). Place one of the rounds on a greased baking tray, add all your filling and spread evenly, leaving a 2cm edge. Brush the edge with a little water, place the second round on the top and press the edges gently together to seal the bread.

Brush the top of the bread with some olive oil and sprinkle lightly with sea salt flakes, taking care not to oversalt the bread. Bake in the oven for 20 to 25 minutes until golden brown. This rock'n'roll beef sandwich is perfect to take on a picnic.

COUSCOUS SERVES 4-6

Now, some people say couscous is so boring that you need to say it twice. However, if you're into this Moroccan staple, and we are, it's a great, versatile flavour carrier. The odd thing is that in Morocco they never serve couscous as an accompaniment to a tagine, and we think that's daft because it's brilliant for mopping up the gravy.

This is a simple recipe for couscous as a side dish. Feel free to use it as a replacement for rice, potatoes or pasta.

225g couscous
2 tablespoons olive oil
300ml hot vegetable or chicken
   stock
a knob of butter

Put the couscous in a bowl and stir in the olive oil until all the grains are coated.

Add the stock to cover the couscous and then cover the bowl with clingfilm. Wait for about 10 minutes until the couscous swells and absorbs all the stock.

Once the stock has been absorbed, fluff the couscous up with a fork.

When ready to serve, melt the butter in a pan. Add the couscous and stir gently, allowing the couscous to heat through and fluff up.

Season to taste (carefully because the stock contains salt) and serve.

Now, this is just the start of your adventures with couscous. At the butter-in-the-pan stage, you can add whatever you like. Try mushrooms, nuts, garlic or sultanas, it really is up to you. If you like the taste of something, then add it and experiment. Best of luck!

MOROCCAN SPINACH SERVES 4

A great warm vegetable dish that can form part of your Moroccan salad table, this is quick and easy to prepare and fab with fish. You'll crack eggs like Popeye after eating this. Don't forget, it must be eaten warm.

25g butter
1 tablespoon olive oil
2 onions, finely sliced
1 teaspoon ground cumin
500g fresh spinach, washed
juice of ½ lemon

In a large wide frying pan, melt the butter and oil. Add the onion and cook for about 4 to 5 minutes to soften.

Add the cumin and cook for 30 seconds or so over a medium heat to bring the flavour of the cumin out.

Add half the spinach to the pan and cook for about a minute, moving constantly so it wilts. Add the rest of the spinach and cook for a further 2 minutes.

Add salt and pepper to taste, then add the lemon juice. Serve immediately.

LEMONADE   MAKES 1 LITRE

This is the real deal – none of your overfizzed, chemical burp juice. The perfect drink for a summer's day, the vanilla gives a cream-soda vibe and it's so tasty and natural too!

8 lemons
1 vanilla pod, split
500g caster sugar

a bunch of fresh mint, chopped (keep a few sprigs back for a garnish)
ice

Take the zest off four of the lemons and set aside. Squeeze the juice out of the eight lemons and set aside. This will make the kitchen smell lovely.

Pour 500ml water into a saucepan, add the split vanilla pod and lemon zest and bring to the boil. Add the sugar and dissolve and simmer for 10 minutes to infuse to make a syrup.

Pour another 500ml cold water into the pan and leave to cool completely. Add the reserved lemon juice.

Add ice to some large glasses and stir through the chopped mint. Pour over the lemonade and pop a sprig of mint on top. If the taste is too strong for you, mix it half and half with sparkling mineral water.

Now, down to the nitty-gritty. This is lovely with a big shot of either vodka or tequila in it. Gosh, anyone for tennis?

SPICED PEARS IN HONEY   SERVES 4

The Moroccans use a lot of honey in their deserts, which is a good thing because we love honey and it's healthy (when have you ever seen a sickly bumblebee?). Well, let's be a busy bee and get on with it. This is a lovely pud and the sweet but spicy pears are great with a dollop of good vanilla ice cream.

juice of 4 oranges
75g runny honey
zest of ½ lemon
1 vanilla pod
¼ teaspoon ground ginger

½ cinnamon stick
½ star anise
4 pears (Williams are best
  for poaching), peeled
50g toasted flaked almonds

In a saucepan, heat the orange juice, honey, lemon zest, vanilla pod, ginger, cinnamon and star anise. When it's boiling, add the pears. Reduce to a simmer, cover and cook the pears, turning them occasionally to make sure they are evenly coated, for about 10 minutes until tender.

Remove the pears and boil the syrup without the lid for a minute or so until the liquid has reduced slightly.

Place the pears on a plate and dress with the spicy syrup. Garnish with the toasted almonds.

Serve with vanilla ice cream or, also good, a spoonful of crème fraîche (the sourness goes really well with the sweet pears).

RICE PUDDING AND JAM PARCELS

MAKES 12 LITTLE PARCELS

Apparently rice pudding has become trendy again, but blow that, we've always eaten it. This recipe is taken from a traditional Moroccan dessert called **rouzz bi halib**, which are filo pastry parcels filled with rice pudding. We've added a dollop of jam and a few more spices.

75g pudding rice
600ml whole milk
70g sugar
2 cinnamon sticks
1 vanilla pod, split
1 tablespoon sultanas

1 teaspoon orange blossom water
1 (400g) packet of filo pastry
a jam of your choice
1 egg, beaten
vegetable oil, for deep-frying
icing sugar, to decorate

Put the pudding rice, milk, sugar, cinnamon sticks, vanilla pod, sultanas and orange blossom water in a saucepan and simmer for 45 minutes over a super-low heat until the rice is cooked.

Set the pan aside and allow the rice to cool completely (this can be left overnight). Remove the cinnamon sticks.

Carefully fold out your filo pastry and cut in half lengthways. Place a hazelnut-sized ball of your cooled rice-pudding mixture at one end of each strip of filo, leaving naked bits of pastry either side of your mixture so you can fold it over to seal the parcels. Add about ½ teaspoon jam to your pudding mix and begin to fold and form your triangular parcel. Take the bottom left corner of the pastry and fold over to form a little triangle at one end of the strip that creates an envelope of ricey loveliness. Then fold this triangle on top of the strip to form a rectangle. Keep folding the triangle until all the filo has been used up.

Just before the final fold, brush your edges with the beaten egg to seal up your parcels. Place in the fridge for half an hour to seal them really well before frying.

Heat a deep-fat fryer to about 180°C or heat a saucepan of oil on your hob. When it is very hot, cook the parcels for 4 to 5 minutes or until golden brown.

Dust the parcels with icing sugar and serve with ice cream or cream (be careful, though, because the insides will be hot – don't scald your gob).

INDEX

HUGE THANKS TO

Top of the list must be John Stroud and Vikram Jayanti, our producers and directors. The series has been as big a part of their lives as it has been of ours. Thanks, guys, for encouraging us to let rip with more madness and, as we say, 'just giving it a go'. We have seen and eaten the world together and we couldn't imagine doing this without you.

Penguin, how lucky we feel to be working with you in making this beautiful book. We are really proud of it and we owe you so much for the work you have all done to produce the book that carries our names. Thanks, guys and gals. Super big snogs to Camilla, our editor; you are special to us and you're a biker too! Much gratitude to Chris Terry, whose photographs can even make us look canny. Thanks also to John Hamilton, Tom Weldon, Sophie Mitchell, Sarah Fraser (creative genius), Kay Halsey, Sarah Hulbert, George Atsiaris, Helen Eka and Pat Rush.

Huge thanks and respect to Sam Squire, one of the best chefs going. We know we have been lucky to work with you. The recipes in this book are great and the times we spent together creating them will remain some of the most memorable in our lives. Thanks also to Danny Richards, who came to help and turned out to be one of the top chefs in the North and a firm friend.

Our extended family: the crew and production office people. Well, we have seen and done so much together, it's a bit special. Thanks to Dave Rea. He is not only one of the cleverest cameramen going, he's a top shooter and a good friend. Remember the whales, Dave. To Dave Keene, who has also been there since the beginning – a top bloke. Thanks and hugs to Nicola Preston, our line producer, even if she does have an unhealthy fascination with Chas and Dave. She is our little Cock-er-nee. Thanks to Simon Weir for joining us – you are a pleasure to work and be with. To the lovely Jules, nothing is ever too much trouble for you . . . good-looking too. Thanks to Mike Snaith, our associate producer, and Marcus Mortimer, partner in Big Bear productions, the backbone of the business. A big thank you to all our fixers and movers overseas who made everything work so well. Special thanks to our new best mate, Steve Patterson, a biker and a diamond.

Lots of love and thanks to our publicist Anya Noakes, a very special lady. Anya's world is always a haven.

Big thanks to all at PFD, especially our agents Maureen Vincent and Charles Walker for their support. Thanks to our very own Perry Mason, Jed Leventhall.

DAVE: I will always be grateful for the goodwill of the people who have spent time writing emails, talking to and laughing with us at book signings and at events. There are some smashing people in this world. I would like to thank my friends and neighbours in Barrow-in-Furness for being the salt of the earth. A big thank you to my mate Dr David Easton, who picked me off the road after I fell off at last year's Mad Sunday, and the doctors and staff at Noble's Hospital on the Isle of Man for putting me back on my feet. I would like to thank Si's wife Jane and his sons Alex, James and Dylan for letting their dad come out to play.

SI: I, too, would like to thank all the great folk who have emailed, stopped us in the street and encouraged Dave and I on our travels. It is always a lovely surprise and very flattering – thanks, everyone.

Thanks to three great mates who happen to be my sons. I really could not be away from you all for so long if I didn't have your fantastic words and texts. I am proud to be your father.

Thanks to Si Harrison for his continued madness and as a constant in my life that can be relied on, no matter what – thanks, mate. To my fantastic Mam for never knowing where the hell I am in the world and costing me a fortune on my mobile phone.

And to my big brother and sister, a big, big thanks.

All my mates, you know who you are, for your love and affection.

And finally, my partner in crime, Dave Myers, for his support and skill with a crêpe bandage – thanks, mate!

And please remember that people, no matter where they live or what they do, are mostly kind in heart and deed. We have found this throughout our travels.